The Myth of Your Addiction

How to release the false self

JoJo
PUBLISHING

DR JEANETTE GREEN

The Myth of Your Addiction
Dr Jeanette Green

Published by JoJo Publishing
First published 2011

'Yarra's Edge'
2203/80 Lorimer Street
Docklands VIC 3008
Australia

Email: jo-media@bigpond.net.au or visit www.jojopublishing.com

JoJo Publishing

Editor: Mandy Naylor
Designer / typesetter: Chameleon Print Design
Printed in China by Everbest Printing

National Library of Australia Cataloguing-in-Publication data

Author: Green, Jeanette.
Title   The myth of your addiction : how to release the false self / Dr Jeanette Green ; editor, Mandy Naylor.

Edition: 1st ed.

ISBN: 9780980871029 (pbk.)

Subjects: Substance abuse.
             Substance abuse--Treatment.
             Compulsive behavior--Social aspects.
             Compulsive behavior--Treatment.

Other Authors/Contributors:
             Naylor, Mandy.

Dewey Number: 616.86

Contents

Dr Jeanette Green was born in South Africa, is of British descent, and is now an Australian citizen. She has lived and worked in both the health and academic professions in the United Kingdom, South Africa, the Middle East and Australia over the last 40 years. During this time, she has been married and adopted step children, travelled extensively and made friendships with many interesting people of different cultures.

Armed with three postgraduate qualifications, including a Master of Science in Rehabilitation Counselling specialising in drug and alcohol and criminal rehabilitation, 40 years of medical experience, 15 years of study of Buddhist philosophy and counselling, and her own personal experience of alcohol addiction, Dr Green decided to write this book.

The Myth of Your Addiction comprises an eclectic approach of western psychology, Buddhist philosophy and personal anecdotal experience of Dr Green's journey to freedom from addiction. It aims to assist those with emotional pain and addictive behaviour reach a state of awareness so they too can be released from their suffering. It is designed to help the reader absorb the principles and practices needed to obtain and maintain freedom from addiction.

Introduction

As humans we love to escape life's difficulties. We will do anything to avoid uncomfortable and painful situations. Habitual procrastination is probably the most common avoidance trait, but we may also develop habits, inherited and/or conditioned, that if performed over long periods of time become who we are and shape our personality and behaviour. Behaviours that become habitual and/or addictive, such as indulging in food, drug and alcohol abuse, gambling and sexual abuse, can begin to erode our normal daily functioning.

According to the fourth edition of the American Psychiatric Association's *Diagnostic and Statistical Manual of Mental Health Disorders*, the medical definition of the word 'addiction' is: preoccupation with a behaviour and/or substance that is prolonged and compulsive; tolerance as one requires more to create the same effect; dependency when one suffers psychological and/or physical withdrawal when the substance or behaviour is removed; and finally, debilitation, when one is no longer able to work and experience healthy relationships, one's finances are exhausted and self-esteem is non-existent.

Long-term recovery from any level of addiction, from minimal scapegoat behaviour to full-blown addiction, needs an holistic approach that incorporates an ongoing interaction between the addicted person's physical, psychological, environmental and social dimensions. This involves: family, who may be experiencing problems of their own, so often overlooked due to concern for the addicted individual; the medical fraternity, for any necessary medications and counselling; and group and community support. As any recovering addict will attest, anyone can give up an addictive behaviour, the difficult part is being able to live a contented life without the addiction.

Learning to enjoy what we should be doing will keep us from returning to our addiction, but how do we accomplish this feat as an individual? We need to create a way of mind or consciousness that encompasses a different state of awareness, an awareness based on reality with a concept of self that is in sync with reality. Only a change in state of mind or consciousness, coupled with medical, familial and community support, will maintain long-term freedom from an addiction. It is the process of reaching this state of new conscious awareness or enlightenment that forms the essence of this book.

As addicts, we tend to live with a mythical and imaginary view of self, mentally, emotionally and physically, that we believe is reality. The more extreme our false sense of self based on deluded beliefs, the more we will suffer when faced with life's difficulties. Our addictive behaviour in response to life's challenges serves only to defend and protect our misconceived self; the addictive behaviour becomes a conditioned, reactionary and habitual response, based invariably on an emotionally painful past that contaminates and eventually destroys the now.

If our current and addictive perception of self feels real, there must be some error or pathology in our perception of actual reality as viewed by others without addictions. It is this false and unreal perception of life, conditioned by familial, cultural, environmental and life-choice experiences, that requires changing. How do we accomplish this? We use the mind, as it is the mind that created the problem in the first place.

As quoted by Einstein:

No problem can be solved by the same consciousness that created it.

We need to be awakened to the idea that our current conditioned form of thinking, and therefore conscious awareness, is unreal. We need to create a new conscious awareness so that we can make choices based on reality thinking, which in time lessens our need for addictive behaviour. Once we realise we are living a life of illusion, we are able to take responsibility for our addictions. I have called this book *The Myth of Your Addiction* because your addiction is a myth and it totally belongs to you. It is your choice, whether conscious or unconscious, to continue with your habitual and addictive thinking and behaviour or begin to live reality.

The following chapters describe a process for realising who you really are and how you can experience reality without the need for addiction. Our true self, forever present, reflects reality but is masked by our conditioned false self. This deluded self, conditioned by genetic predisposition, familial and life experiences, hides our fears and insecurities and creates a mythical world in which we feature as the central 'I'. This separate and selfish style of living leads to emotional and physical suffering that we then compensate with habitual and addictive behaviour.

My personal thoughts and feelings as a former full-blown addict due to a very misconceived self, and my gradual awakening from a life of non-reality, infiltrate this writing, which describes the process or journey to the elimination of my addiction. My study and practice did not bring instant enlightenment but did bring a gradual awareness and understanding that I was living an unreal hell, a non-reality based on my conditioned past.

Old habits die hard, and as long as they are perceived to be enjoyable, whether deluded or real, the addiction will persist. Knowledge, awareness and particularly painful feelings that begin to erode our non-reality alert us to our suffering. In some cases, unfortunately or maybe fortunately, our emotional suffering coupled with addictive behaviour can reach a point where the addiction becomes pathological or full-blown. We cannot continue with the addiction short of becoming very sick or dying. At this point, some individuals prefer death rather than surrender their addictive thinking and behaviour.

The only escape from our emotional suffering and addictive behaviour is to use the mind; we need to change our thinking and feelings of our perception of self. It is our conditioned mind that underpins our addictions and perpetuates our current dysfunctional behaviour and suffering. Our addiction can become our saviour, as it alerts us to our unreal existence and we are able to seek an alternative and contented mode of living without the need for addictive behaviour.

A mentor and close friend of mine said years ago that the longest journey he ever took was from his head to his heart. I had a vague understanding of what this meant at the time, but only today can I perceive what he was really saying. Reaching an awareness of his true self was what he was describing; he had eliminated his false self with all its emotional suffering and addictive behaviour. It is this mental state of awareness and contented being that this book will assist you to experience: a realisation of your true self. Once realised that as an addict your exaggerated concept of self is no more than a delusional mental image of who you perceive yourself to be, you are able to release this false self. You stop living in your compulsive and possessed mind with unreal emotions that lead to addiction and instead begin to live the essence of who you truly are without the need for compensatory, addictive behaviour.

As Einstein said:

The true value of a human being is determined primarily by the measure and sense in which he has attained liberation from the self.

Chapter 1

The myth of your addiction

What is an addiction? There has always been controversy over which addictive behaviour can be legitimately diagnosed as an addiction. Most of us think of addiction in terms of substance abuse, such as drug and alcohol abuse, which invariably goes hand-in-hand with psychological problems, physical degradation and crime. Not only does substance abuse cause extreme suffering to the individuals concerned and their families, but it also has an impact on society.

There are also many other addictions that we use to alter our mood or behaviour, such as gambling, shopping, eating, working, sex and criminal abuse. There is wide cultural variation as to which of these addictive behaviours are socially acceptable and the amount and type of substance considered appropriate; for example, western culture condones alcohol for recreational purposes whereas Islamic culture forbids it for any purpose.

Addiction can be seen as a long-standing compulsive behaviour. All of us have addictions of varying degrees; we may overeat, smoke, watch TV or surf the internet for long hours. Some of us are addicted to drama or excessive work; we may enjoy chaotic lives, or in sheer contrast we may prefer a life of apathy and become a couch potato. Excessive power can become an addiction, which can be seen in dictatorial leaders of certain regimes. Others may be addicted to possessions, money and excessive risk-taking, reflected in the world's current fiscal scenario and the number of bodies on the slopes of Mount Everest.

Addictive behaviours and the use of addictive substances under appropriate conditions are generally approved. It is when the behaviour becomes pathological and changes from habitual desire or craving to being psychologically and physically injurious to ourselves or others that it is labelled 'full-blown' addiction by medical and administrative bodies.

As humans we certainly have the capacity to deceive ourselves. We create a story in our heads (our script) to define our concept of self in order to justify our actions and cope with our perceived daily stressors. We find this easier to do than confront and deal head-on with the realities of life's challenges, however painful they may be. This tendency towards self-deception erodes our psychological and social wellbeing, which can lead to irrational thinking and addictive behaviour if extreme. Why do we wish to avoid reality? Actually, it is not reality we are avoiding but the uncomfortable emotions induced by our perceived stressors and our reactions to them.

We are inclined to memorise all our experiences along a continuum with intense emotional pain at one end and intense pleasure at the other, so that all our memories are experienced as pain or pleasure of varying intensity. We can observe this in highly emotional people, especially gamblers, drug users and compulsive sex addicts, where the initial euphoria dominates all future addictive behaviour as the addict tries to recreate the same initial sensation, the ultimate high of that first 'hit'.

Whether consciously or unconsciously, we chose how we wish to experience life and its many challenges, crises and sufferings. We may chose to escape and lead a life of addictive drama, or completely fail to lead a life, never waking up to the meaning of life. One thing we do know is that most addictive behaviours are a way of coping, with the behaviour developing during our early formative years, often due to an underlying psychological disorder.

Studies have proved a concrete correlation between smoking and depression. When a smoker quits, there is a drop in the happy hormone, serotonin, which often leads to carbohydrate cravings as a compensatory measure and subsequent weight gain. Another example is the feeling of panic that accompanies alcohol withdrawal, part of which is associated with low levels of serotonin. Having an early morning drink after a heavy night, or 'hair of the dog that bit you', to alleviate these feelings is unfortunately a behaviour that only compounds the cycle of alcohol addiction.

This conditioned and reactive coping response to life lacks awareness; it is carried out almost unconsciously, as most addicts will attest when in the grip of full-blown addiction. The compensatory behaviours of smoking, drinking and gambling, just to name a few, are performed in unconscious mode. Have you ever wondered how the drink, cigarette or chocolate you're about to savour arrived at your lips? You went straight from the negative emotion, which you think is invariably caused by someone else, to the alleviating behaviour without thinking, conscious choice or awareness that the behaviour is not conducive to your mental and physical health.

Why are we unaware of our destructive emotions and resultant behaviours? It is because we are so caught up in our unconsciously-created mental and emotional script of how we perceive ourselves that we incorrectly believe is our reality. We genuinely feel emotional pain and are always in fear of what life might present due to our continuous inner dialogue, that little voice inside our heads that only serves to compound our unreal story. We cannot be unhappy without a story about ourselves to make ourselves sad. This inner dialogue, based on emotional memory of current and past experience, good or bad, defines our concept of self. We therefore deal with life's problems through a fictitious script of self based on fictitious emotions; an emotional story we have unconsciously created of how we perceive ourselves.

Common examples include getting angry or impatient with others because we feel threatened, or going on a shopping spree to alleviate a negative mood. As written by Elizabeth Lesser in her book *Broken Open: How Difficult Times Can Help Us Grow*, addiction, secret love affairs, and journeys into the underworld of passion and sexuality are the stuff of myths. If these myths are habitually played out, they become addictive behaviours that can be injurious to ourselves and others if taken to the extreme.

It is the accepted norm for us to seek security, love, fulfilment, validation and pleasurable activities, invariably based on our memories of the past and anticipation of the future. Our thoughts and feelings are therefore continuously preoccupied with our past and future in an attempt to secure our perception of self, without which we feel we exist. Our beliefs, based on ancestral, cultural and actual conditioned experiences, create a perception of self that we feel justifies our current behaviour. Our conditioned beliefs, created by a conditioned mind, allow us to live unreal emotions based on unreal mental scripts and thoughts. It is this conditioned mental script that we unconsciously and erroneously believe is reality and who we are. Anna Nicole Smith comes to mind as an example in that she created her delusional script of Marilyn Munroe to escape her childhood pain and lived that script literally to her premature end. Another example could be a man who valiantly goes to war and imagines he will never be killed. Thus begins the myth of an eternal and separately perceived self, with all its accompanying emotions. That is our reality, but we could not be further from the truth!

We unconsciously believe that this mythical ideology of a mind-projected future secures freedom and happiness. Is this true freedom? It is a delusional script created by the mind that conjures an imaginary identity of self but at the same time distorts and obscures reality. The greater our misconception of self, the more extreme our behaviour in response to normal day-to-day situations. All our emotions, positive and negative, are therefore completely integrated as part of our perception of ourselves. If you insult someone, they may immediately become angry because their perception of self, or 'I', thinks it has been attacked and they feel hurt. When we are angry we certainly don't rationalise why we are angry, we just react in a hurt way towards the person or object we think has caused this hurt. Our response may be verbal or, if we feel sufficiently hurt, physical.

Paul Eckman, a professor of psychology at San Francisco Medical School, University of California, explains how our brains learn negative behaviour in Daniel Goleman's book *Destructive Emotions: How Can We Overcome Them? A Scientific Dialogue with the Dalai Lama*:

> *The first time one acts in a really cruel fashion may be the most difficult. But if you continue to act in a cruel fashion, you are in all likelihood changing your brain so that cruelty now becomes your temperament and cruelty becomes your way without thought or reservation.*

This perception of being a separate self appears to be the source of all our emotional suffering. It is this unconscious, conditioned, habitual and reactive behaviour to our perceived threatened self that underpins all our addictions. Does this 'I' really exist or is it just an illusion based on a continuously transforming unconsciousness perception and reaction to what is? How can the perception of 'I' truly exist beyond our thoughts?

Obviously there are tremendous differences among people and how they respond to similar situations. Some individuals regularly feel strong negative emotions such as anger, jealousy, greed or hate, while others are less vulnerable to these emotions. We can already see a difference in cultures. Some definitely appear to have a calmer set-point to which they rapidly return after a traumatic event in their lives. Whether this is genetic and/or culturally determined or both is open to discussion. What a difference it would make to our lives if we were to become continuously aware of our deluded and negative thoughts and emotions and were consciously able to evaluate them as they occurred? We then could be responsible for each thought and emotion when it began, rather than becoming hurt by someone then getting angry and lashing out.

Even now, the Alcoholics Anonymous (AA) saying of 'One drink, one drunk' has been challenged by a national survey conducted by the American National Institute of Alcohol Abuse and Alcoholism, according to the *Scientific American Mind* article 'Big myths in popular psychology'. This study revealed that 18% of one-time alcoholics could drink in moderation without abusing alcohol, and that behavioural training programs in which moderate drinking is the goal are at least as effective as the Twelve-Step Program of AA. However, this finding is highly controversial and it is important to add that such tactics don't work for everyone. For those with a long history of pathological drinking, abstinence programs are the best way to go.

Unfortunately, it is a common western assumption that our emotional programming is set at birth and that we can do little to modify destructive emotions that occur in response to life's challenges. Western psychology views conscious awareness, or the perception of self, as part of the mind and therefore as inborn and programmed, while eastern philosophy views the conscious perception of self as an awareness independent of the mind. Traditional knowledge through the ages, from Buddhism to the Bible and the Koran, has enlightened us as to the malleability of the mind and thus our emotions. There is also now medical and scientific proof to support the notion that we can change our thinking and thus our emotions regardless of our inherent habitual and addictive dispositions.

The conscious mind comprises sensory perceptions of memory, thought and feelings that create the perception of 'I', an awareness of identity and existence. This existing perception of a separate 'I' creates a feeling of continuity that allows us to perceive and feel who we are in the moment. It is this perception of self, whether real or deluded, that dominates how we experience daily events and our behavourial reactions to these.

We perceive all external stimuli through our senses, which create the perception of an experience. This perception is then compared to the memory of any previous, similar experiences and then judged as liked or not liked. An idea about it is formed from this and the concept is banked to memory. Any distressing thought, unresolved problem or painful childhood memory is often suppressed by the mind, waiting to manifest later in response to life's challenges. It could be just a feeling of anxiety or full-blown anger that triggers it, depending on the situation and how it resonates with the earlier suppressed experience. It was Carl Jung, a well-known 20th century analyst, who labelled this past memory the 'unconscious mind' or 'shadow'. This 'shadow' unconsciously provides continuous feedback to the conscious perception of self and waits as a hidden entity until the trigger moment arrives for it to manifest.

So, as you are beginning to understand, we are totally connected to our past, and not only our past of yesterday and of childhood but, more importantly, the past of our evolution. Our so-called current mental awareness or consciousness is not only due to our environmental conditioning (nurture), but also our evolutionary and hereditary conditioning (nature). It contributes to our emotional DNA blueprint of who we are in mind and body. There is the argument of 'nature versus nurture', but it is the input of both nature and nurture that creates a perception of self that can either align with reality or can be so far removed from reality that the person appears insane. How I see myself (my perception of self), how others see me and who I really am can be infinitely diverse, never to relate, or they can be one and the same when we are in touch with our true being of reality.

As long as we identify our perception of self with external qualities such as our possessions, appearance, social role, successes, failures and religious and political beliefs, we will suffer. This deluded, mind-made perception of self is unreal and will cause us to feel insecure, threatened and vulnerable. We will therefore always be seeking more success or failure, for example, to validate and bolster our misconception of self; we have made our success and failure who we perceive ourselves to be; we have totally identified with the success or failure; we have become the success or failure. We will therefore defend this misconceived self and seek new experiences, good or bad, to reinforce this identity and create the feeling that we truly exist.

It is the underlying feelings of anxiety and insecurity as a result of a misconception of self that we attempt to alleviate with compensatory addictive behaviour. This can be seen in any excessive, habitual and/or obsessive behaviour performed either individually, such as drug and alcohol abuse or sexual predation, or collectively, such as in political power, corruption, family feuds and wars. It is this unconscious myth of perception that leads to our unconscious myth of addiction with its only-too-real suffering. Therefore, no addiction can be eliminated until we comprehend and gain a conscious mental awareness of the source of our addiction.

My addiction was alcohol. It was an easy choice in a family with an ancestral and current history of alcoholism. A fellow member in AA once said, 'No decision in our family was made without an alcoholic drink.' It was much the same in mine; the blueprint was already present psychologically, if not genetically and physically. Alcohol was readily available and consumed in the home, especially at the enormous parties my parents regularly held. I enjoyed the taste of sweet sherry dregs at the bottom of a party glass around the age of four. Little did I know then that my Scottish and Irish ancestors had literally drunk themselves to death, with one aunt dying from neat gin consumption.

Alcoholism and other addictive behaviours have dominated my immediate and extended family worldwide to the current generation.

I was born hyperactive and always felt the need to excel. My identity comprised my looks, figure, IQ, successes, relationships, sexual prowess and, finally, my alcoholism. I was mentally and emotionally attached to it all. They were all who I perceived myself to be. I also believed others perceived me exactly the same way. I could not have been more deluded!

Having been born into an already dysfunctional and alcoholic family, I certainly inherited a predisposition for alcohol physically, mentally and emotionally. The behaviour escalated over the years, and with increased physiological tolerance to alcohol exacerbated by a 20-year marriage to an alcoholic and continuous psychological repression of any ill feeling or anxiety, I developed full-blown alcoholism at the surprisingly late age of 45.

My alcoholism only compounded any feelings I already had of not being good enough. I was unconsciously carrying my past and compensating any painful feelings with conditioned behaviours that only increased my suffering. My inherited genes were well conditioned. I even identified with my addiction, especially when labelled the 'Detox Queen of Sydney' as a regular rehabilitation occupant, inclusive of my excessive physiological tolerance to the drug Valium, used to counteract the withdrawal effects of alcohol. I derived my complete sense of self from the story going on in my head (my mental script) rather than from what was actually taking place. It was ceaseless, an illusion, a deluded sense of self that I believed was my reality but was actually very far removed from it.

I adopted false masks and defences, maintaining a full-time academic university post with all the modern day trappings. All this resistance was still masking the fear I felt and I remained ambitiously driven to compensate any feelings of inadequacy with acquiring six degrees, various jobs, travel, buying houses, and accumulating money, as well as disastrous attempts to compensate with alcohol. I finally came to the realisation that nothing would or could compensate the ever-present feeling of discontent.

As Eckhart Tolle says in his book *The Power of Now: A Guide to Spiritual Enlightenment*:

You will not be free of that pain until you cease to derive your sense of self from identification with the mind, which is to say from ego. As long as I am my mind, I am those cravings, needs, wants, attachments and diversions and apart from them, there is no I.

It is this mind, conditioned by our hereditary, familial and environmental past (nature and nurture) that creates how we perceive ourselves today and how we imagine others view us. How could we possibly know how others view us in terms of our achievements, wealth, relationships, or even our failures? Such is our addictive thinking.

Our deluded sense of self is like compound interest: we enhance any feeling initiated by the mind with repeated negative and scripted thoughts. There is a constant feedback between mind, feeling and emotion, which then affects and justifies our current behaviour. For example, if someone is driving me absolutely crazy I might reach for the cupboard and have another drink. We never feel real contentment because we are constantly seeking a feeling of being something, achieving something or are trying to eliminate a nasty feeling to create a sense of comfortable existence. Our constant feeling of unease and/or fear, based on conditioned memories of our past experiences, is creating our future so that we never truly experience the now.

This imaginary 'I' is an illusory sense of self based on memory. It is a conditioned belief system nourished by experience. We therefore unconsciously attract experiences, both positive and negative, to reinforce our personal beliefs, hopes and fears and to validate our existence and continuity of our deluded perception of self. For example, a woman might think 'I am happy because I am beautiful' or 'I am unhappy because I am ugly'. We sometimes hear the words 'You are not your body'; that is, we are not the mental pictures or feelings we have of our bodies. Unfortunately, these mental images are how we imagine others are viewing us, which is not assisted by the society we live in today that seems to monitor, judge and exploit our every move. In fact, we are our bodies, not in terms of body perception and feelings, but we are our bodies in terms of all our senses. A true sense of feeling, seeing, hearing, smelling and touching in the now, without any past mental conditioning, is pure awareness and reality. It is an awareness that stimulates our senses alone, and not the imagination we use to create the deluded perception of who we think we are or who we think others think we are, none of which is real.

The western world is totally enslaved by identification with material possessions, achievements and relationships, not only physical enslavement but also psychological and emotional enslavement. The mind not only initiates thoughts but also emotion, which is the body's feeling or sensory response to the mind. Covert emotional enslavement is not always so immediately obvious but is the underlying cause of alleviating and compensatory addictive behaviour.

Robert Powell quoted in his book *The Great Awakening: Reflections on Zen and Reality* from the 1948 Bombay talks of the famous Indian philosopher Krishnamurti:

The mind is its own prison, therefore, transformation and liberation from suffering can only be achieved by ending the ceaseless activities of the mind.

An example is an individual who has been in an abusive relationship, never allowing themself to enter into another relationship lest it should turn out to be the same. By doing this, the individual is condemning themself physically and psychologically to a life of imprisonment. As stated in a proverb in the Old Testament of the Bible, 'As you think so shall you be.' Your thinking creates feelings and emotions based on past experiences which then perpetuate a cycle of who you perceive yourself to be.

A quote from *A Course in Miracles,* by the Foundation for Inner Peace, aptly describes how our sense of self functions from moment to moment:

We look inside first to decide the kind of world we want to see and then project that world outside, making it the truth as we see it. We make it true by interpretations of what it is that we are seeing and we are using these perceptions to justify our mistakes, our anger, our impulses to attack, our lack of love in whatever form it may take. We will see a world of evil, destruction, malice, envy and despair.

Just look at current world terrorism: heinous behaviours resulting in horrendous atrocities to innocent people carried out by individuals who are living their extreme version of a deluded self, often culminating in death. In any society and culture there will always be extremists, good or evil. Extremist behaviour can be viewed as a form of addictive behaviour. As in the case of any addiction, such as sexual predation, substance abuse or criminal behaviour, certain ground conditions (nature and nurture) need to be cultivated and conditioned.

The forensic psychiatrist Dr Michael Welmer stated in an interview on the American television show *Larry King Live* in May 2007:

We first have to acknowledge that evil behaviour is a disease or illness so that the pathological psycho-physiology can be intervened earlier. Evil behaviour, needs to be seen as a psychological illness or disease, which is any defect in the structure of our bodies or personalities that prevents us from fulfilling our potential as human beings. Although alcoholism and drug addiction are now classified as diseases, the alcoholic and drug addict still appear their own worst enemy, much the same as the terrorist becomes his own victim.

Extreme and conditioned beliefs can become ideologies so strong, inherent from birth and conditioned from an early age, that they can become an individual's total identity. Armed with an ideology and often from poor or marginalised environments and conditioning, the recent world terrorists use their belief to support their illusion of self, both individually and collectively. Their past conditioning has become their future and they die without experiencing reality; they die with the illusion of martyrdom. Even an extreme behaviour, if deemed by society to be good, becomes acceptable to society, as seen in marginalised people living under totalitarian, non-secular governments with strong religious ideologies and sectarian fighting, especially in the Middle Eastern countries of Iraq, Pakistan and Afghanistan, and African countries of Somalia and Ethiopia. Another example is the extreme and collective military response by the USA to protect what they think may happen in the future. As Madelaine Albright, a previous US Secretary of State, was heard to say, 'Disgrace with the US is almost a disgrace with God.'

Are the suicide bomber, drug gang murderer and US soldier who kills others for their beliefs any different from each other? As much as the terrorist strives for security with an idealist religion imposed on others, and the west responds by imposing its ideology of free values on others, we appear not to realise that this is a collective and deluded perception of all our insecurities and fears. Now we have a collective perception of fear fighting a collective perception of fear. How insane?! This is human insecurity versus human insecurity. But once caught up in our misconceived self and its habitual and/or addictive behaviours, such as food indulgence, drug and alcohol abuse, sexual predation, and even terrorism and war-making, we cannot possibly perceive that it is our own mind that is the root cause. And minds create communities and communities create governments.

The myth of your addiction originates and ends with you. Only you can change your life script based on your concept of self by changing your thinking and starting to live an authentic self rather than the fictitious one created by your mind.

As quoted in *The Great Awakening*, Krishnamurti said:

For the mind which is the known and the product of the past, to dissolve is the very opposite process. It means the cessation of all seeking, all thought, all the mind's activities in the nature of clinging or grasping are directed at self-assertion.

We now begin to understand that our addictions are based on unreal thinking and unreal feelings; that it is our misperception of self, or myth of self, that feeds our addictions. How do we slow the mind and cease its addictive thinking and behaviour? We cannot just eliminate or forget about what's happening in the world, our job, or our family, although some of us make a very good attempt at it with our addictive behaviours. We need to let go of our unreal memories of experiences, feelings and beliefs that create the illusion of what we incorrectly think and feel we want, need and believe to be our reality. It is our feeling of 'I', an unreal 'I' that supports the sensory feeling and security of who we believe we are. The sense or perception of 'me' is not real as it is based on an unreal feeling of fear. We all experience our personal problems but they do not need to become our identity. They are not who we are, they just reflect life situations.

Acceptance of life's difficulties would allow us to experience less pain rather than remain ignorant of the fact that our problems belong to us, which invariably attracts more drama and therefore more pain. Cultivated by hereditary factors, family, environmental input and conditioned thinking, this evolutionary, psychological and conditioned cycle of addictive behaviour is not easily broken. A realisation of the illusion of one's life may be instantaneous but changing the conditioning takes time or is never reached. The closed loop feedback circuit of negative thought and feelings needs to be opened to break the cycle of a deluded perception of self, which can only perpetuate a life of unreality and suffering. This happens to some people spontaneously, while others break the cycle of years of drama with an horrific incident or tragedy that causes them to examine their life and change. Despite repeated incidents, others continue with their pain and suffering until the day they die. For some addicts, there comes a point when they realise that external compensations will no longer fulfil their underlying fear of insecurity, vulnerability, anxiety and panic that dominates daily life and leads to their seeking addictive behaviours.

As stated by the Grand Taoist Master Hua-Ching Ni in his book *Entering the Tao*:

The superior man knows what should be known by him.
The sick one does not know what should be known by him.
The one who is sick of being sick therefore can be free from being sick.

It is only by complete acceptance of 'what is' and the willingness to change, combined with the willingness to accept the help of others more spiritually advanced, that we are able to forgive ourselves and our past and others and their past. The essence of all religions is a willingness to surrender to God, a Higher Power or Grace rather than surrendering to 'I will', the perception of self dominating one's daily life. It is no use analysing our thoughts as it is the mind-created thoughts that are the problem in the first place. We need to dis-identify from the mind and have the willingness to surrender to a higher authority, God if you will. This can only take place once we begin to realise and become aware of our inherent pathological thinking, feeling and behaviour. Only then can we begin to heal and live reality rather than a misconceived perception of self, a non-reality that perpetrates our addictive behaviour. We need pure sensory awareness in the moment to truly experience reality. The actual experience and perception of the experience need to be the same; perception of the experience should not be different based on past conditioning.

As quoted in *A Course in Miracles*:

Nothing real can be threatened. Nothing unreal exists. Herein lies the peace of God.

That is a profound statement because it is only through our mythical view of a false self that we incorrectly perceive we can be threatened. Nothing unreal exists because whatever we imagine ourselves to be is an illusion. The misconceived self is unreal and does not exist, and if we don't identify with this false sense of self we will experience mental and emotional peace. Herein lies the peace of God.

In summary…

- Addiction arises due to an unreal perception of self, conditioned from birth, with which we identify thus creating a fictitious life script.

- We unconsciously believe our perception of self to be real, unaware that it is an illusion, out of touch with reality and the source of our addiction.

- Addiction is therefore created from unreal thinking and unreal emotions in response to living; it is based on unreality.

Chapter 2

Addiction

The word 'addicted' means 'physically dependent on a particular substance'. The word 'addict' means 'a person who is addicted to something' and originated in the 16th century when it was used as an adjective to mean 'bound or devoted'. It comes from the Latin *addicere* or 'to' + 'say' (*Oxford English Dictionary*). The term 'addictive personality' taken literally means that an individual possesses certain habits or traits that describe the distinctive qualities of that person.

Society today still holds perverse ideas about addiction, which include anything from being mad, neurotic, psychopathic or having a disability. As recently as the 1970s, alcoholics and drug-abusers were often committed to mental institutions and/or jail in order to deal with their problems, which were unacceptable to their families and society. Alcohol and drug addictions are now viewed as diseases, therefore shouldn't other addictions such as eating disorders, gambling, shopping, sexual abuse, emotional abuse, criminal acts and, questionably, terrorism be classified as diseases? And what about addiction to work, control, suffering and drama? The individuals concerned have all given themselves up to a particular behaviour.

As quoted by the well-known physician Harold Urschel in his book called *Healing the Addicted Brain*:

> *Addiction is a chronic physical disease that attacks the brain…. Unfortunately, addiction-related brain damage is not a quick come, quick go disease…. Often there is an underlying psychiatric disorder…. Only new medications… combined with behavioural therapy and twelve-step programs will push up the success rate.*

Denial or a non-acceptance of an addiction will continue as long as the perceived gain of the addiction appears to outweigh the suffering caused by the addictive behaviour. Everyone's level of suffering is different, so at what point does an individual decide they have experienced sufficient suffering and seek help, aptly termed 'rock bottom'?

A year ago I phoned an old friend in Sydney, also an alcoholic, the son of two eminent doctors and a potential doctor himself except for his destructive drinking habits. He had diabetes, had experienced previous episodes of pancreatitis, and now had a blockage in his bile duct and was turning yellow. His words were, 'I am still drinking.' Three weeks later he was dead; his suffering never outweighed what he believed was the short-term pay-off of his continued drinking. Was his psychological pain so bad that the physical pain as a result of drinking was still a relative form of relief?

There are many factors that influence our behaviour, such as our inherited traits, and our environmental and cultural background, including societal ideologies and influences. All addictions have physiological, psychological, sociological, environmental and even financial inputs, all of which need to be included in terms of the myths and theories of the cause of addiction and, in particular, rehabilitation.

Health and welfare professionals have certainly assisted in defining the diagnostic and therapeutic measures for the presence and severity of an addiction. Current American Psychiatric Association criteria for addiction in the fourth edition of the

Diagnostic and Statistical Manual of Mental Health Disorders (DSM IV) include: the preoccupation with a substance and that preoccupation is prolonged and compulsive; tolerance of the substance, meaning that larger and larger doses are needed in order to produce the same result that normally requires a smaller dose; dependency and withdrawal symptoms, both physical and/or psychological, when the use of the substance is abruptly discontinued; physical, psychological and social debilitation so that normal functioning is significantly impaired.

The above signs and symptoms are not exclusive to substance addiction, such as drug and alcohol addiction. While sharing a room in a rehabilitation centre, I have seen a gambler, abstinent from gambling, have the same panic attack and withdrawal symptoms as I was having from my lack of alcohol. Even the notorious Green River serial killer, when asked why he sexually assaulted and murdered so many women, replied that it was because he craved more and because he could.

Any addictive behaviour can replace the words 'substance abuse' and may appear as an illogical, obsessive and compulsive behaviour to eat, drink, take drugs, sexually abuse or even kill, especially when the behaviour physically and psychologically harms the addict and others. The medical model tends to emphasise genetic predisposition and physiological causes for addiction. These underlying causes may need medication, temporarily or permanently, to repair brain balance and assist recovery, similar to a progressive disease, but the participation and influence of the psychologically conditioned, subconscious mind cannot be ignored.

Speaking from personal experience as a full-blown alcoholic, I believe total reliance on the disease theory of addiction needs to be regarded with some caution, as the power to heal comes from within. Complete reliance on rehabilitation centres and community groups such as AA, which play an extremely important facilitating role, do not provide the whole answer to recovery.

Addiction is a choice initially, an unconscious choice based on our past conditioning, and genetic, environmental, physical and psychological factors. More emphasis needs to be placed on the psychology of addiction, with its initially hidden emotional correlates. Addictive behaviour often manifests minimally as habitual and covert scapegoat behaviour that may develop into a more extreme overt addiction, such as alcoholism, which then goes on to include pathological, physical and psychological behaviours.

There will always be rationalisations and excuses to maintain an addiction, from the irate husband who blames his family and continues to drink, to the suicide bomber who regards westerners as infidels in the name of his religion. Both are processes, conditioned and cultivated by hereditary disposition, environmental, physical, psychological and sociological inputs, and cannot be seen just as dysfunctional behaviour.

All addicts, whether the alcoholic at the pub, the heroin addict scoring in the alley or the terrorist planning a bombing, invariably associate with other individuals or groups with similar lifestyles and addictive behaviour. This is the psychology of addiction; some behaviour is just more extreme than others.

Today's society certainly condones the consumption of alcohol and use of certain drugs as a way to relieve stress, regardless of the significant rise in addiction among all cultures. The ready availability of alcohol and recreational drugs, let alone prescription drugs, has increased both resistance and tolerance as regular consumption becomes more acceptable.

Almost all races have consumed alcohol for thousands of years, with the exception of the American Indian, Maori and Aboriginal people. Some cultures and/or religions forbid the use of alcohol; for example, Muslims and, to a lesser degree, Jews and the Chinese. Not surprisingly, we see less incidence of alcoholism in the latter groups today, whereas Aboriginal, American Indian and Maori societies have been ravaged by the introduction of alcohol.

We cannot be sure where familial inheritance ends and environmental conditioning begins (nature versus nurture); it is most likely a mix of nature and nurture that contributes to addiction. For example, the American Indian's reaction to alcohol is inherited and individuals instantly become addicted when they consume alcohol, whereas others may have a slower-developing predisposition to an addiction, conditioned by cultural, familial and environmental influences.

Cigarette smoking, now directly linked to lung cancer, can also be viewed as a psycho-physiological disease due the smoker craving nicotine.

I feel that medicine does not adequately deal with addiction, especially as most addicts strongly deny that they bear some responsibility for their addiction, such as advanced lung cancer patients who still smoke or patients with fatal skin melanoma who continue to use sunbeds.

It has been suggested that addicts have chemical receptors that produce exaggerated cravings for more, but this is currently disputed by research. Research has shown a correlation between depression and addiction, but to what degree is this psycho-physiological, pathological, hereditary and/or conditioned? New drugs such as Campral and Vivitrol have been scientifically proven to assist alcoholics in repairing chemical brain balance and reducing euphoria if they lapse and drink again, but they cannot remain on these drugs permanently. Every drug has long-term side effects, just as the original addictive substance of choice.

As humans we tend to avoid emotional disturbances, having been conditioned to feel that life without crises equates to normality and stability; however this is not the case. It is our ability to cope with crises that keeps life real and stable. Our inability to cope creates emotional attachment to our crises, such as mid-life crisis, menopausal crisis, unemployment crisis, divorce crisis and death crisis, and we incorrectly perceive that this is who we are. We identify and become our crises. Some people appear to cope better with crises than others; this is because they accept and face their reality, however painful. Others try to escape reality with avoidance strategies of habitual and/or addictive behaviour, whether physical and/or psychological. Individuals who are spiritually mature have an awareness that any confusion, anxiety or uncertainty they experience is not who they are but simply life situations and part of human existence.

The majority of people today live according to other people's values of how things should be. They are prisoners of the known, and the known is nothing other than a prison of the past. A mind-made identity is a total myth or imagined self based on mental attachment to a belief system, invariably conditioned. I remember chatting to a 25-year-old man serving coffee to subsidise his college tuition in Sydney. He said that if he didn't have a degree, a deposit on a house and a car, as well as a potential wife, by 25 years of age he would become one of the marginalised and underprivileged members of society. This is conditioned thinking; the imagined self is removed from actual reality and life is conducted in a bubble of illusion that we think is reality. This man would be no less a person without all of the above trappings of western society, but the conditioned belief system with which he identified created his perception of who he was.

Members of any community and/or religious group cope well with their crises by supporting each other, but there are always some in the group who totally identify with the group ideology. Their belief then becomes an obsessive, addictive ideology serving the ego, rather than an ethical and moral way of living. It is in these situations that addictive behaviours manifest not only individually but collectively. The addiction may not be to a substance such as food, alcohol or drugs. Any rigid belief system can lead to addictive behaviour. This can be observed in so-called cults such as the Ku Klux Klan, a religious racist cult, the Children of God, a religious child-sex cult, and the People's

Temple, a mind-control cult that led to mass suicide in Jonestown in 1978. Members of such cults exhibit irrational behaviours and even mass suicides as a result of conditioned, deluded thinking. Our deluded perception of self therefore remains vulnerable, insecure and defensive, always ready to defend and react when threatened. It is this unreal thinking, accompanied by unreal emotions, that we then attempt to escape and alleviate with our habitual and/or addictive behaviour.

We now know that feelings and thinking are correlated with inputs from our hereditary past (nature) and environmental determinants (nurture). It was Carl Jung who first suggested that environmental factors were not the only determinants as to how we behave but that evolutionary and hereditary factors provide the blueprint of conscious behaviours. We are linked with our past, not only the past of infancy and growing up but, more importantly, with the past of our species and ancestry. We cannot help noticing history repeat itself, particularly when it comes to suffering. For example, a fear of something can easily develop if the predisposition to feel fear already exists in the subconscious. Many individuals live in fear of being attacked; it is something that they cannot control. Others don't even entertain the notion as they are aware they cannot control extreme addictive behaviour. Have you ever tried rationalising with an alcoholic?

Personally, from my earliest memories, I have never been without a sense of unease and anxiety. I am now aware that this is an underlying fear which was inherited (nature) and conditioned (nurture) during my formative years. My entire, immediate and extended family were highly intelligent, driven and of nervous disposition. There was the means to alleviate our anxieties: our beautiful mahogany alcohol cabinet always came with us wherever we lived.

Consuming alcohol was socially acceptable, entertainment acceptable, professionally acceptable and even medically acceptable. I believed using alcohol was a normal part of life and that every other family in the world consumed the same amount of alcohol in their homes. Therefore, with my predisposition for anxiety and a substance to alleviate it, my alcoholic conditioning began early. There was always the feeling that things were not quite right, particularly when it came to the dynamics of relationships in our family. Not knowing any better, and armed with an inner feeling of something missing, I coped by using alcohol until the age of 18 when I finished school and left home permanently.

Encouraged to achieve, I did so with a good education, but it was also okay to drink. The phrase 'Never trust a man unless he drinks' certainly existed in my thinking, surrounding social and professional relationships. I certainly identified with a group: intellectuals who drank. Needless to say, I was always in the pub after work with lawyers, lecturers, teachers and doctors, all of whom had the same group identification. It was okay; we were not the hobos you see walking down the street or lying in the gutter with a bottle. I now know that although we believed we had an air of respectability due to our achievements and education, what we were doing was really no different from the guy lying in the gutter, just our collective misconception of self thought it was!

Alcohol was accepted by my peer groups; that was my identity; they were my mentors, they were my friendships. This falsely created identity, cultivated by my surrounding stimuli and with the additional habit of alcohol changing the chemistry of my physiology, removed my view of reality completely.

I pushed on, working and living overseas, attracting the relevant experiences initially to bolster my delusional ego until the balloon popped and I had to admit defeat; I had become my addiction. It took years of busts and rehabilitation, AA attendance, a postgraduate degree in counselling, the study of Buddhist philosophy, great teachers, mentors and friends, including voluntary service, to reach the awareness I have today and, in particular, a contented life.

I find it somewhat incongruous that I am now working in the strict Muslim state of Saudi Arabia at the age of 59 years, but there is a lesson here too: it is called 'Inshallah', which in Arabic means 'God willing'. This is a daily reminder of 'Thy will not mine'. I need to remain in touch with my real self and not live life through my unreal self with 'I will' being in control, which would lead to the return of my alcohol addiction.

As previously stated, we mentally register all our experiences with feelings of pain or pleasure. It is the intensity of the emotion that remains with us and is responsible for triggering and maintaining our addictive behaviour; for example, a heroin addict who is always seeking the pleasure of that first high. Therefore, the emotional pain or pleasure of any experience is primarily psychological, but that does not mean that biological factors and other environmental inputs are not involved. For example, internet porn and gambling are not only both addictive for many but also billion dollar industries. What we do know is that the memory persists, a memory of the pleasure, and if triggered it will again attach to the feeling and emotion produced by the original behaviour or substance. It is this pleasurable feeling, arising from behaviours such as drinking, eating, gambling and sex, that becomes so important when managing our addiction.

Research has indicated that the eating disorders anorexia nervosa and bulimia are both addictive behaviours used to manage stress and/or depression, as stated by Dr Michael Oberschneider, an eating disorder psychiatrist, on *Larry King Live* in May 2009. There is also a proven correlation between smoking and depression; the nicotine appears to have an antidepressant effect. Feelings of panic accompany alcohol withdrawal, which research suggests is correlated to serotonin levels in the brain. The latter I have experienced many times and, while I do believe there is a chemical base, I have observed that the intensity of the withdrawal experience was highly correlated to my mental and emotional state at the time.

We cling tightly to our notion of self, conditioned from past experiences, and when conditions in the present do not meet the expectations of how we perceive things should be, we suffer. Our expectations are thwarted and so we react to the situation, thus compounding emotions that we then attempt to sooth with habitual pleasurable behaviour that may become addictive. We are all guilty of avoiding taking responsibility for our behaviour because we wish to avoid the negative feelings and emotions associated with the consequences. We all experience life's pressures of discrimination, racism and sexism for example, which can cause us to withdraw from life's challenges because the choices are too difficult. As someone once said, today's world is all quantity and velocity, but where is the quality? Often the more pain we feel, the more driven we become and the more we live in our illusion of an unreal self with pain-avoiding strategies and/or addictive behaviours.

On questioning an eminent psychiatrist specialising in substance abuse and addiction as to whether he thought people could alter their serotonin (happy hormone) levels in order to rationalise further addictive behaviour, he responded, 'I don't think we as humans are that clever.' But personally I think we are! We develop, live and become our deception of self, albeit unconsciously, with our deluded rationalisation to maintain our unreal thinking and feeling that supports our addictive behaviour. Even my husband said, 'I love the feeling of the control–release cycle,' as he addictively worked, didn't work, drank, didn't drink. He eventually became his control–release cycle in everything he did. His blood pressure was high and sexual function diminished when we parted, as a result of this cycle.

Our mental prison is usually represented by something to which we are excessively attached, such as our behaviour, possessions, roles, a person, a dream or a fantasy. The forensic psychiatrist Dr Michael Welmer commented on *Larry King Live* in May 2007 that suicide bombers are completely ego-driven and often feel betrayed by society and vengeful. It is easy enough for a down-and-out 22-year-old to be a perpetrator of a heinous crime in the name of his religion because his Matawa (religious priest) and existence from a young child permitted it.

We are now aware that our addictive thinking, with associated feelings and emotions resulting in various kinds of addictive behaviour, has physiological, psychological, sociological and environmental roots. All of these components determine the outcome.

Bateson's 1968 theory of a cybernetic (feedback) approach, where the mind is seen as part of the environment, predisposes an ongoing interaction between the individual, the physical environment and social dimensions. No dimension is able to be considered in isolation; all are part of the whole. Cybernetics aims to present human behaviour in terms of a self-correcting mechanism that is a closed-loop feedback system. Within it, information flows between the conscious mind, our emotions, our actions and the environment, not forgetting the unconscious mind, which appears hidden but influences our thoughts.

As quoted by Calvin Hall and Vernon Nordby in their book *A Primer of Jungian Psychology*, Jung said:

When the ego and the shadow are in close harmony, the person feels full of life and vigour, therefore the nature of the shadow can be equally effective whether it is promoting something evil or something good but it is always there, waiting to step in with little resistance from the weakened ego. It has tremendous staying power and never really surrenders.

We all have this feedback circuit of feeling, memory, desire and action; the stability of the feedback, in terms of ourselves in relation to the environment and therefore our daily equilibrium and coping skills, depends on whether it acts self-correctively or goes into runaway mode. Skewed conditioning of thinking and emotions, coupled with already dysfunctional hereditary inputs, can lead to rapid onset of an addiction with a rapid deterioration in an individual's behaviour. Insufficient or excessive gain in certain areas will finally cause the system to reach runaway mode. This latter stage can be compared to an addict's final stage of full-blown addiction, where the mind and body, now pathologically damaged and unstable, require increased input of addictive behaviour and/or substance to survive. It is this adapted mind–body system that then lives a modified or false reality, short of terminating altogether in death. Hence the idea that an alcoholic may feel sobriety is wrong in some way and intoxication feels right. Recovering addicts, initially sober, often feel saner than the people around them and find the situation intolerable. They are aptly labelled the 'dry alcoholic', which is not a contented sobriety. If it is this false perception of sobriety that drives us to drink, then this perception must be pathological in its thinking.

Until this vicious cycle is interrupted, the competition between addictive behaviour and the perception of self will continue and the sincerely deluded individual will continue with his or her addiction. Forced intervention may temporarily resolve the situation, but this is not always the case and then the individual returns to his or her addiction and potential death. The addict, no matter what type, holds a false notion of self and self-control. It is only through an understanding of the misperceived self that they are able to release their deluded thinking, feelings and compensatory addictions. Only then will they learn how to relate to the world through a less-threatened view of self and live a normal life.

One thing we can change is our thinking: how we think or how we don't think. The addict, with his or her instant gratification of thoughts and feelings, needs to take responsibility. We cannot be absolved from taking some responsibility for our addiction, even though heredity factors and painful experiences may influence our feelings. An holistic view such as the cybernetic model, which suggests an ongoing interaction between the individual, their environment and relationships, could assist. What religion, philosophy or way of life could possibly encompass all of the above? The answer is one that incorporates mind, body and the environment in a single experience; being able to experience equanimity, or being at one with others and reality. All religions, in essence, encompass this philosophy and try to teach us that we are at one with each other, reality and the universe. The more at one we are with what is, that is, acceptance of what the universe provides instead of exerting our will on the universe, the more in harmony we will be with ourselves and with others. Again, 'Thy will not mine.'

Addiction manifests in every sector of society, whether in the form of drugs, gambling, pornography, crime or terrorism. Psychological pain is an inherent part of the human condition because the deluded perception of self is repeatedly in conflict with reality, which leads to self-deceptive and depreciating behaviour. We can argue that all addictive behaviours are bio-psycho-social spiritual disorders. Carl Jung succinctly stated, 'Neurosis is always the substitute for legitimate suffering.' The psychologist Eric From defines it as a process of 'learning to like to do what we have to do'. Too many of us lead a life of suffering, caused by our selfish desires, irrational fears and deluded view of self. How do we remove this pathological circuitry, continuously redefined by society? How can we possibly find our freedom and peace in the very myth of life itself? The answer is that we have to let go of self-deception, our mythical view of self. Only then will we be able to contact our innermost feelings and understand the nature of our true selves; an understanding and acceptance that both pleasure and suffering are an inherent part of human existence, and an acceptance of what is because it already is.

In summary...

- Addiction is a choice, initially unconscious, which is conditioned by genetic, environmental, physical and psychological variables and inputs.

- It is the psychologically conditioned perception of self, with its pathological thinking and emotions, that triggers, feeds and maintains the physical addiction.

- The addiction becomes who we are; we live our false sense of self with the deceptive belief that we are coping with life.

- Society views addiction as a compulsive and chronic physical, mental and emotional disease with the addict in a state of denial or non-acceptance that their behaviour is injurious to themselves and/or others.

Chapter 3

The myth of self

So who am I? And how do I perceive myself and my existence? As humans we have been conditioned to experience ourselves as isolated individuals, dependent on an external environment to provide feedback that we really do exist. Without this feedback of continuous stimuli we tend to feel non-existent. We enjoy the perception of a separate and special self and perceive everything else as 'out there', to which we react in order to defend our perception of self.

'Selfing', as quoted by Kabat-Zinn in his book *Wherever You Go, There You Are*, is that inevitable and incorrigible tendency to construct out of everything and every situation, an 'I', a 'me', a 'mine', and then operate in the world from that limited perspective, which is mostly fantasy and defence. We tend to see ourselves as the centre of the world rather than a part of it, a perception that in the extreme can lead to cynicism and suffering rather than compassion and kindness.

Our perception of self comprises many coats, which we wear for different situations thus forming the basis of our personality and habitual and/or addictive behaviours. The external inputs contributing to our perception of self begin with our genetics and our conditioning from early childhood; whether we experienced a loving childhood or an abusive one, it moulded our beliefs, our concept of self and how we behave today.

Imagine three corners of a triangle: how I view myself (self perception); how others view me (external perception); and who

I really am (my true being). The further apart and more diverse the three corners are from each other, the further removed I am from living reality and the greater my suffering. This is due to the fact that the perception I have created of myself, that is, the story in my head, is not in sync with what is actually taking place, therefore my assessment of situations will be biased or downright skewed. The closer the three corners are to approaching a point focus, the more likely I will be living reality.

If I feel sorry for myself and experience suffering, it is because I do not have the slightest inkling of who I am. I have become totally identified with my thoughts and feelings of how I perceive myself and do not see myself as others see me. I only perceive and feel myself based on my personal story in my head with all its cravings, desires and fears. I therefore overreact in response to events and people's actions, seeing them invariably as a threat to my perceived existence by viewing every situation through a selfish and deluded view of reality.

This self concept acts as an imaginary filter, based on past memories and experiences, which contaminates my present behaviour leading to repeated suffering and addictive behaviour. An example of this was my inability to pass large trucks at speed on the highway without having a panic attack due to a previous unfortunate experience with an irate truck driver at night and in poor weather conditions. Although I no longer suffer panic attacks, I still dislike highways congested with traffic and, in particular, large speeding trucks!

Examination of my extended family and ancestry found most members were strong-willed, driven and in a constant state of agitation except when compensating their state with alcohol or pills. My ancestors, paternal and maternal, were nearly all alcoholics; this was my predisposition and conditioning. From my earliest memories, my friends didn't think as fast, run as fast, or swim as fast; I found them slow and boring, and when it came to my teachers in elementary school, I felt they were even worse.

My intolerance of others started early and with it my perception of self as different and separate. I didn't show it; I only felt it at the time and obviously did not share it.

Although of European descent and classified 'white' in the then apartheid system in South Africa, I had a tanned skin and curly black hair which did not assist my concept of self during my formative years. My only memories of love and attention were from a Zulu boy who worked for us and could neither read nor write, and a permanently inebriated maternal grandmother who I found to be great fun. Granny was a chronic 'topper upper' alcoholic who lived to 97 years of age on three bottles of brandy per week and packets of cigarettes. She kept herself comfortable; I thought that took pretty good intelligence!

My upbringing at home in South Africa was somewhat conditional. My parents expected me to excel so they could be proud of me, and were happy for me to drink as long as I didn't embarrass them. Nearly all of their contemporaries from the little town of Bloemfontein, where I spent my early years, died in their late 60s, mainly through alcohol consumption.

My perception of self was as 'unworthy' or 'not good enough', and I ventured forth into the world trying to prove my worthiness. But who was I? I hadn't a clue. How did others see me? It didn't even enter my mind. I existed totally in my mental picture of who I felt I was at any moment. I was completely attached to my own mental view of self, totally mind-identified. Ready to prove myself, validate myself and receive validation from others, I worked hard and received rewards but still had an inherent feeling of 'not quite good enough', which created an imaginary fear of others and how they would judge me.

My self-perception could be represented by two sides of a coin: achievement on one side and nothingness on the other. I called it my 'feast or famine' self. Even when I excelled in some way, such as by obtaining a PhD or having a loving relationship, I still had a feeling of being undeserving. Moments of elation were short-lived and I had a continuous feeling of unworthiness and lacking, which I attempted to dull with alcohol which only temporarily quelled my anxiety.

Without questioning my behaviour, I ran from one compensation to another, from one success to another, from one failure to another, from one pleasure to another, from one suffering to another. I resigned myself to this state of being as inevitable, unaware that I was totally deluded. I was living a fantasy life, which was totally out of sync with reality. My misperception of self not only compounded an already inherent nervous disposition but also increased my fear and feeling of separateness from the world.

Armed with a good education and a driven and disciplined work ethic, I continued my false life of qualifications, full-time work, marriage and travel. Although at times I was very successful both financially and in my career, and had a large social network, I didn't know anyone intimately and felt very alone. One thing I did enjoy, to which many other addicts will attest, was the control–release cycle, with its highs and lows associated with addictive behaviour. It supplied me with a sense of existence without which I felt invalidated and non-existent.

The type of addiction we have is influenced by the variables of our genetic predisposition, environmental conditioning and perceived experiences. Mine were all alcohol-based. As they said in rehab, I didn't stand a chance!

The perceived self creates our so-called personalities, which influence the way we act and behave in response to everyday situations. Our concept of self is nothing but a thought and emotional product of a conditioned past and a conditioned memory. We believe we are separate entities and protect ourselves by reacting against anything that attempts to menace our existence. This inherent belief gives rise to negative emotions and behaviours due to a chronic and deep-seated feeling of fear. This habitual and deluded view with which our minds identify is not reality but a skewed view of it, which then causes all of our suffering. We therefore live in a mode of constant expectation, invariably thwarted due to our concept of self being out of sync with 'what already is'.

We might think we are living in the present moment, in the now, but we are not. We are living concepts of our past that we have brought into the now. Our future has already become our past and so the pattern repeats itself with each new experience. As Dr Phil McGraw has repeatedly discussed in his television programs on addiction and in his book *Self Matters*, the track record of your past behaviour is a very good determinant of what your future behaviour will be. For example, if I have previously alleviated my suffering with alcohol at the end of a bad day, there is a good chance I will do it again.

Most of our energy comprises mental activity with which we identify and reference our past so that we remain psychologically and physically imprisoned in our habitual and addictive thinking, feeling and behaviour. We have very little understanding of who we are and why we behave the way we do. Our concept of 'being' is an extremely deluded self comprising a mind and body that are in continuous agitation and act as a barrier between our true self and reality. This feeling of a separate 'me' existence is a dualistic form of thinking, a false sense of self that validates and leads to a separate concept of 'me'.

Hubert Benoit stated in his book *The Supreme Doctrine*:

Man believes in the utility of his agitation because he does not think that he is anything but that personal 'me' which he perceives in a dualistic manner. He does not know that there is in him something quite different from this visible personal 'me', something invisible which works in his favour in the dark.

It has been proposed that our intellectual energy previously used for environmental adaptation and sustaining our existence is no longer needed for present-day physical survival. This now excess mental energy tends to be used for continuous validation of the self, creating an illusory identity so that all of our happiness and pain occur in an unreal world of our own thinking and making.

Krishnamurti as quoted in *The Great Awakening*, stated:

Beyond the physical needs, any form of desire for greatness, for truth, for virtue becomes a psychological process by which the mind builds the idea of me and strengthens itself at the centre.

Our intellectual energies are the source of our sufferings, particularly in the case of addiction, where they begin to undermine our functional existence. We only have to look at the suffering caused by psychosomatic and physical addictions in society today. It is almost as if our thinking has become too specialised and has lost its spontaneity, vitality and adapting process. I believe continuous analytical and addictive mental activity to the exclusion of everything else underlies many of the diseases incurred today. We tend to neglect ourselves, ignoring what is happening to our bodies. We don't attend to our emotions, and when they become too uncomfortable we look for a quick fix that then becomes habitual and/or addictive. We attempt to escape from reality mentally, physically and emotionally, thus turning our negative energies towards ourselves.

We all inherit a genetic predisposition of one sort or another that needs to be triggered or switched on. Unfortunately, the genes of some diseases are turned on when we are born, whereas others need the sensory and physical input of conditioning and repeated behaviours over time to manifest as a disease or full-blown addiction. To quote a friend, 'My mother developed Alzheimer's on the very next day following the fatal shooting of my son.' Her stress and suffering had become too much to bear. Possibly years of stress accompanied by genetic input and childhood conditioning tripped her genetic switch for the onset of this disease. As most addictions are now regarded as disease, they require the conditions to be switched on either spontaneously or over a period of time, depending on our conditioning and genetic input.

Due to our limited concept of self and associated negative emotions, we are constantly seeking a feeling of security and the stimuli to provide this feeling, unaware that our perception of self is a self-made illusion. We are conditioned into living a 'myth of self', a separate self that in reality does not exist but mentally is constantly compared to what the material world 'out there' demands we should be.

Television and other media bombard us with images of thin and beautiful women. No wonder anorexia is not only on the rise but appearing in girls as young as 8 years, and there are now teen girls desiring plastic surgery. Another example of the myth of self is the suicide rate for Australian farmers being disproportionate to the normal population suicide rate. The loss of farms that have been in the family for generations as a result of an extremely long drought is taken personally by the farmers; the farmers are identifying with the failure of their farms.

Our misperceived feelings of separateness, aloneness and unworthiness are compounded by our repetitive, negative, self-created thoughts of what we perceive we 'should be'. We then create compensatory behaviours that become habitual and/or addictive in an attempt to reduce or eliminate negative thoughts and emotions of anxiety, anger and fear.

Society today uses and somewhat condones addictive behaviours until they become destructive or injurious to our welfare. We devote much of our time to temporary satisfaction, desiring more and more compensations to alleviate our feelings and sufferings. Even a belief in an after-life and UFOs can create good feelings as they support the idea of a more meaningful existence, but these feelings are still mind-made and temporary. Who is to say they are real or not? Carl Jung, the well known psychologist, felt that the apparition of UFOs must be a symbol produced by the unconscious self to compensate and fill the void or empty feelings we experience. I remember a friend who was a recovering alcoholic and gambler becoming obsessed with UFOs during his early sobriety. Had he perhaps exchanged a physical addiction for a psychological addiction?

My study of Buddhism was initially a compensatory mechanism until I experienced a realisation and incorporated the teachings into my daily life. I then began to take responsibility, living the essence of Buddhist philosophy rather than just mentally identifying with the philosophy, which only enhanced my notion of self. Even proclaiming to be an atheist is a belief or ideology that in some cases is probably just serving the ego.

As Carl Jung states in his book *Flying Saucers: A Modern Myth of Things Seen in the Skies*:

A myth or the myth of self is essentially a product of the unconscious and therefore a symbol such as a UFO requires psychological interpretation…. For primitive man, any object, for example, an old tin that has been thrown away, can suddenly assume the importance of a fetish.

This effect is obviously not inherent in the tin but in the mind of the individual. We live entirely in our imagination and all of our strivings, aims and objectives are mind-made, correlating our identity with our imagination and nothing else. Our self-imposed deadlines and goals, with their temporary satisfaction, only provide transient moments of fulfilment. We never question the origin of our false self with associated thoughts, feelings and behaviours as we move from one compensatory event to the next, thus never really experiencing real contentment.

This type of thinking, which is completely reliant on external stimuli to create and reinforce the concept of self, is deceptive and does not reflect reality. We are unaware that our addictive behaviour arises from the desire to enhance and validate our false concept of self and incorrectly perceived existence. This is caused by ignorance as a result of fear of losing our feeling of existence; we fear death of the ego or mythical self. We have no understanding of how to contact our innermost feelings of who we really are. We live a lie, a dream world of our own making, a dream concept of self, living a non-reality instead of an awakened concept of self, in sync with reality.

For example, are women who fall in love with high security inmates 'acting out' in their seeking for fulfilment and wholeness to compensate for whatever is lacking in their lives, such as the men who don't pay them attention or the men who aren't in their lives who they feel would make them whole? The prison inmate is a constant; he can't move and has to listen, and his distinct 'less than' concept of self that he has previously 'acted out' reflects her 'lack of' at the extreme level. Both individuals are severely deluded in their attraction for each other; a compensatory relationship that is both symbiotic and dysfunctional.

As quoted in *The Great Awakening*, Krishnamurti stated:

The only difference between the average natural man and the man who is given to daydreaming is one of degree; the latter is merely an extreme case of the former…. The thought comes about when experience is insufficiently understood, giving rise to a 'psychological residue' (clinging to some habitual conditioned thought pattern). The psychological residue or memory gets revitalised when challenged by the present, giving rise to the illusion of the self and the suffering ensuing from that concept or idea.

We tend to judge every experience, object and individual through our feelings of attraction or aversion, based on our memories of the past, in order to maintain a personal mental identity of who we think we are. Our view of self therefore never accepts 'what is' but continuously uses past experience (our dislikes and likes) to evaluate the now. This leads to continuous dissatisfaction because there is a resistance to what already exists, due to an imaginary expectation based on our past. If we ignore or try to suppress a negative emotion, we only intensify it because we have identified and conceptualised the emotion and made it who we perceive ourselves to be. We remain in a continuous state of reaction, ready to judge each experience and ready to defend judgement by others. This constant anxiety and continuous fear with attachment to our past, our mental baggage, underpins our addictions.

The concept of 'me' conditioned by ancestral, cultural and an experience background serves only to compound any fearful memories with which we already identify, further exacerbating the delusion of a conscious self. With each repeated bad experience that we unconsciously attract, our self-image is diminished further thus compounding our emotional pain. These painful feelings can reach an intolerable point where some form of compensation is needed to alleviate the feelings.

An example is the case of the abused wife never leaving her husband because she feels too frightened and unworthy and is unable to view him as a control freak and abuser, sometimes leading to murder either way. Another example on a lesser scale might be when we have a verbal or physical outburst, or instead keep our feelings bottled up and remove ourselves from the situation so as not to be judged by society. Still feeling angry and insulted or hurt, we may take an alternative route of compensation such as going to the gym (considered fairly normal) or shopping or eating or drink alcohol, all of which reinforce predisposed, conditioned and habitual behaviours.

A good example of my own unreal feelings occurs when I have to make a difficult phone call. Prior to the call, I tend to feel nervous knowing that what has been said previously upset me. This is bringing my past conditioning into the present. I am already in a reactive state, ready to defend my present existence in response to whatever was said. I wrongly perceive the phone call as a threatening experience based on a misconceived memory of the past experience. Each painful experience is labelled, judged and banked to memory so that it becomes a concept with an associated feeling, ready to be revitalised should the moment arise. These thoughts and feelings become easily reactivated and relived just by reflecting on the past, thus further compounding any feelings of 'poor me' and placing me in an even more reactive state of mind for the next phone call.

You can now begin to understand that as long as we identify with the mind's closed circuit of thoughts and feelings, we will continue to alleviate or compensate our feelings with some type of reactive and/or addictive behaviour. As Eckhart Tolle says in his book *The Power of Now*:

We only find relief from our minds when we revert to unconsciousness, which can be induced by sleep, sex, alcohol, drugs and even TV viewing.

I would include in this list excessive work or busyness, and excessive 'woe is me' when we are forever telling our victim stories, thus removing ourselves from the present experience in order to avoid painful or uncomfortable feelings. Tolle feels, as do many others including myself, that if drugs (whether prescription or illegal) and alcohol were not so readily available, most of us would be labelled insane as we would probably resort to other addictive behaviours to alleviate our emotions and anxiety.

So, how are addictions related to our misconception of self? Well, it is similar to dreams: dreams feel very real until we wake up to reality and realise they are not real. The same applies to my deluded self: my perception and feeling of myself is not real although it feels very real, so real that all of my self-limiting, reactive and addictive thinking and behaviour are based on it.

We tend to remain fixed in maintaining our false perception of self, relentlessly identifying with this deluded concept, associated emotions and our addictions. Our past memories are completely integrated into our concept of self, which we repeatedly validate through daily activities, invariably at odds with 'what already is'. The more we identify with this false concept of self, the more removed we are from actual reality. This non-acceptance of 'what is' (reality) and 'what is not' (our false concept of self, which is unreality) causes us to suffer painful feelings that perpetuate further suffering as we avoid facing reality. It is this feeling of sheer panic or just a chronic background anxiety that pervades our daily routine. As a result, we use various habitual behaviours to suppress or eliminate these feelings depending on our current mental state, circumstances, previous conditioning and genetic input.

My form of escape, as previously mentioned, was alcohol. It is the only drug that completely suppresses all parts of the brain at once, but can also result in death if used in excess. Some individuals live just below the line of being manic, on the positive side using their drive and excess energy for great achievements, and on the negative side sometimes ending up 'down the tube'. For example, you only have to think of a few heads of state, artists and geniuses such as Winston Churchill, Ernest Hemingway and Dylan Thomas, all great people but all of whom enjoyed some form of addiction during their lives. I would say I was borderline manic; the psychiatrist actually said I was the nearest to being bipolar without being classified as bipolar. I now know I used drink in order to cope. It took the edge off everything and, as so many alcoholics have proclaimed, it made me feel normal.

As long as we identify with our minds and feel we are nothing more than our image of self, our anxieties and habitual behaviours will continue to the point of full-blown addiction due to our increased need for relief. I now realise that addicts are far closer to finding out who they really are than those who go through life without any addictive behaviour. Therefore, I say to all addicts out there, whatever your addiction, be brave because you are closer to your real existence, your true 'being', than ever before. Your painful existence can alert you to your destructive behaviours.

In summary...

- The perception of self, with all its thoughts and feelings and self-fulfilling behaviours, forms the basis of our personalities; it validates our perceived existence.

- The concept of self with which we so strongly identify is nothing but a product of a conditioned memory of our past; it is not real and yet all of our self-limiting and addictive behaviour is based on this concept of self.

- 'Selfing' is the term used to describe our indulgence of a separate and special concept of 'I'. It is out of sync with reality and causes conflict, drama and emotional suffering which we attempt to alleviate with addictive behaviour.

Chapter 4

A matter of perception

How do we perceive things? Physically, we have five senses: seeing, hearing, smelling, tasting and touching. Seeing and hearing are paramount for human interaction, although research has proved that smell also plays a large part. If we walked into a room of strangers without a preconceived mental image or emotional concept of self, we would not experience any pre-judgements or expectations. We would perceive the strangers as just a bunch of people, of whom we are one and the same. That is reality. Unfortunately it is not usually that simple because we all carry around a mental and emotional concept of self that affects our perception of everyday events. Note the feeling or emotion you have next time you walk into a room full of strangers, even if it is just the supermarket.

Each time I am invited to moderate or speak at a conference, I request in advance all the speakers' names, histories and abstracts of their presentations in order to be 'over-prepared'. Frightened of making a fool of myself, I cover every possible scenario to avoid any uncomfortable situation eventuating. This is due to my concept of self having to be perfect, conditioned over many years by parents who always maintained an external image of perfection so as not to reveal any shortcomings in the family household. As a family, we carried a perception of self that obviously felt less than our perceived standard of how we felt we should look, act or behave. We may be able to intellectually rationalise that all is okay but still have an emotional distortion that all is not okay, completely unaware of the source that triggers our skewed and delusional concept of self.

Dr Michael Oberschneider, psychiatrist and director of an eating disorders clinic in the USA, said on *Larry King Live* in May 2009, 'The genes load the gun and the environment provides the trigger.' Certainly we are genetically programmed before we are born, and there is now proof that we have genetic predispositions to certain personality traits, such as shyness, hyperactivity and apathy. This is prior to our development of a mental consciousness, conditioned by immediate and extended family, school, work, life experiences, etc. From the moment we arrive, every experience, from mother's nipple or lack thereof, is banked to memory; all thoughts and associated feelings and emotions are stored in our subconscious with an already programmed genetic input. You might ask, 'Do we stand a chance?'

I only have to study my family tree to see that I didn't stand a chance: all family members displayed traits of hypermania and there were probably a few undiagnosed bipolar traits, judging from the stories I've gleaned from my relatives. My paternal Ross ancestors heralded from Scotland. They were cloth people who appear to have either drunk themselves to death or drowned in a loch possibly due to inebriation. Others were daringly adventurous, sailing and settling in the far away countries of South Africa, Australia and Canada during the 18th and 19th centuries. The name 'Ross' in Canada is highly correlated with the disease of alcoholism, devastating entire families. In South Africa, they were caught up in various wars and the diamond industry. Considering our contacts with Rhodes, de Beers, etc., I asked my mother where all the money went. Her reply was, 'They drank and gambled it away.'

My maternal Irish ancestry came from County Claire. Hyperactivity and alcoholism plus drug addiction were and still are rife on that side of the family. My maternal grandmother was a direct descendant of Dampier, who discovered Western Australia and was known to be a drunken rogue. Therefore, with a genetic predisposition for hyperactive behaviour and alcoholism, I was not only set up but set myself up for driven achievement on the one hand and a drink on the other.

How we perceive, feel and view ourselves is therefore totally influenced by our past experiences and conditioning, inclusive of genetic input. We don't live reality, we begin to live our distorted view of reality, which we certainly believe and feel is reality. Any habitual or addictive behaviour that we use to reward, remove or escape from uncomfortable emotions caused by our unreal thinking only increases the illusion of self and we then begin to live our addiction; we become our addiction. Our judgement of daily situations, invariably based on past memories, obscures the reality of what is really taking place. This unreal perception is further compounded by a western capitalist viewpoint of what we 'should be'. Unless we have model figures, are highly qualified, and are successful in our achievements and gathering of material possessions, our self concept is perceived as a failure.

Every experience we incorrectly perceive and feel only compounds our mind-created concept of self, which prevents us from experiencing reality. Thinking creates feelings and emotions; it is a closed-loop feedback system where the thinking creates more thoughts and more thoughts create more feelings, both positive and negative.

As humans we incorrectly believe that we are comfortable in the 'known', which is our personal memory of the past. We are always seeking permanency in a very impermanent world, which somehow we seem not to accept. Psychologically and emotionally we feel we need to be someone, strongly supported by western capitalist thinking, which reinforces this 'someone'. We are always thinking of what we should be doing or what we shouldn't be doing, either in the past or future, but never actually living the present. We therefore miss the only real living there is, which is in the now, as our minds are always somewhere else living the movie in our heads. Have you ever missed out on the enjoyment of the moment when experiencing an orgasm because your mind was somewhere else, perhaps planning a future event? Some individuals never experience orgasms because their minds are always somewhere else and never in the moment.

We are forever striving for fulfilment, attempting to make purposeful that which is purposeless in order to avoid any future uncomfortable feelings. An example is the husband striving for directorship because spending time at home with the family is somehow too painful. Righteously and morally we judge every experience as 'good' or 'bad' based on our past, and then mentally identify with the emotion of the situation and turn it into a concept of who we believe we are or should be, thus further reinforcing the deluded and false self.

This delusion of self is a split viewpoint of a perceived separate body that I own and a mind that creates a separate perceptual feeling of 'me' or 'I', when really they are all one. One could not possess a body without a head and therefore a mind, and vice versa. This idea of a separate body and mind is a type of schizophrenia or 'split personality'. An example quoted in many books is the ripples or waves on the ocean that are not separate from the ocean, as the ripples and waves are the ocean, which produces the ripples and waves. In the same way, the world 'peoples' and people are part of the world. Similarly, the experience and the person who experiences the experience are not separate; they are one. We may intellectually understand this but need to feel it, as described in the words of Krishnamurti in *The Great Awakening*:

> *The feeling of separateness, the desire 'to be' is psychologically based on fear, the fear of losing the myth of self, the ego, the personality of who you think you are; the fear of feeling nothingness; the fear that you don't exist.*

We become upset or angry if someone suggests that our problems are unreal and created by the mind and therefore can be healed. The sense of who we feel we are is then threatened, especially when so much personal time and effort has been invested in creating our deluded and false perception of self. We are fearful that our 'me-ness', who we believe and feel we are, will no longer exist. Much of what we do and say is motivated by a fear of losing hold of our perceived self.

It is our mind that causes our negative emotions and suffering, which we then attempt to alleviate with our habitual and compulsive behaviour. This conditioned and narrow view of who we perceive ourselves to be leads to nothing but repeated doubt and repeated dissatisfaction in our daily living. We then attempt to find some external factor to blame for the constant dramas occurring in our lives. External circumstances are not the cause of our anxieties and troubles; our mind, with its habitual and reactive thoughts, leading to habitual and reactive feelings and behaviours, is the cause all of our suffering.

As quoted by Hua-Ching Ni in *Entering the Tao*:

People tend to think that events in their lives are determined by external influences so that they blame their happiness or misfortune on a divine but external authority who arbitrarily imposes punishments and rewards upon them, or they blame their mothers and fathers for either spoiling them or denying the fulfilment of their early emotional needs. Perhaps they think it is their environment which is supportive or hostile toward them, or their racial or educational backgrounds which determines the joy or sorrow which enters their lives. Or maybe they feel their lives are governed by blind chance. Generally, people tend to look no further than the superficial elements which compose their experiences. They fail to realise the deep truth that what appears as external reality is actually only a mirror of their own inner consciousness.

Recently while working at a Middle East eye hospital, the male head of department, who was very good-looking and exceptionally charming, made me feel very uncomfortable in his presence to the degree that I would try to avoid him because so much obvious anxiety would manifest. I was a professional woman of 55 with 35 years of work experience who had lived and worked around the world among many different cultures. Heavens! It only compounded the situation. With a certain amount of awareness on board, I was able to reflect on the situation and realise that my emotions, which felt very real, were a delusion. Why? Because I was associating memorised emotions of painful experiences with authoritative, charming, good-looking men with the present situation.

Most people try to avoid difficult situations, as I was attempting to do. If feelings become intolerable, some individuals medicate these uncomfortable feelings with addictions such as drugs, alcohol, sex or shopping; habits I certainly had previously enjoyed! These temporary escapes only suppress negative emotions. Jung, the well-known 19th century psychologist, labelled these suppressed negative emotions our 'shadow' and said that they would manifest again when we are faced with stressful situations.

Attuned alertness to my emotions made me quickly realise that my perception of the situation with the good-looking head of department was an illusion. Fearful of authority figures, in particular a handsome male with subtle predatory and misogynistic charm, I was emotionally reacting to a completely normal situation by allowing painful memories to contaminate the now. In a nanosecond the mind-identified self can take over, while we remain completely unaware of the situational triggers causing the emotional response. My illusory self had been threatened and the underlying feeling of fear, my 'shadow', had broken through. Awareness of the intensity of my anxiety and awareness of its trigger assisted me in releasing it, with the knowledge that my anxiety was unreal.

As Lama Yeshe stated in his book *Introduction to Tantra: A Vision of Totality*:

We instinctively feel that we exist as something very real, definite and substantial. We have no doubt about this real me and it seems absurd to think of it as just another hallucination. If we take the trouble to search for the supposedly concrete 'I' or 'me', we will discover we cannot find it anywhere, neither in our head, arm, leg or any other part of our body is our 'I'. The same is true of our mind. None of the countless thoughts or feelings that continuously arise and disappear is the real 'me'.

Hopefully we can now begin to understand how our inherent and conditioned misconception of self is the source of many of our problems and addictions. This unreal or illusory perception of self with accompanying emotions distorts our perception of reality, which may only cause subtle harm, or the negative emotions could cause destructive harm, as in the case of full-blown addiction.

The English word for emotion is derived from the Latin word *emovere*, something which sets the mind in motion, whereas the Buddhist perspective of emotion is an obscuring mental factor. Either way, our perception of reality is misperceived. These emotional states not only impair our judgement of situations but also our ability to make objective ongoing decisions and choices.

As stated by Dr Ricard Matthieu, a Buddhist monk and author, in the book *Destructive Emotions*:

Excessive attachment, desire for instance, will not let us see a balance between unpleasant and pleasant, constructive and destructive qualities of someone or something.

I am sure we can all share a time when we were so obsessed with a potential lover or partner that we saw none of their negative qualities until much later, when the relationship was over and we probably wanted to destroy them, thus forgetting any of their positive qualities. We become imprisoned by a certain incorrect way of thinking that either drives us toward something or someone of desire or repels us away from something or someone we hate. It is an exaggerated and/or unreal assessment of 'what is' with unreal emotions. A repetitive negative emotion eventually invades our psyche and becomes our temperament.

We all know the angry, jealous, greedy or dishonest person in our social and working networks; they literally live their emotion. The more limited a view we have of ourselves, the more negative our self-image remains and the more inadequate and worthless we feel. A compensatory inflated concept of self is often protecting a small or fearful 'me', which will invariably sabotage every situation with some reactive type of behaviour due to a feeling of being threatened. Instead of acting objectively, with little or no emotion involved, we react subjectively with an emotional outburst, or we harbour the emotion and deal with it later with a so-called rewarding behaviour.

In the Kingdom of Saudi Arabia where I work, it is compulsory for women of all nationalities to wear an *obeya*, the black coat that covers the body entirely from neck to toe, when out in public. That, coupled with the somewhat demeaning attitude of some Saudi males toward women, particularly at the security and immigration stations at the airport, has led many a female expatriate to visit the bar as soon as they hit Dubai International Airport. We compensate with habitual, reactive and addictive behaviours to hold onto our emotional security, which serve only to compound the already exploited feeling of unworthiness. Initially aware of my emotions, I reached a stage where I would later berate myself for having bothered to respond, let alone allowing the situation to upset me, especially when the people involved are so completely ignorant of their behaviour; that has been their conditioning, to view women as lesser beings and thus treat them as such. Today I view the situation as sad with a sincere compassion for any female treated in such a demeaning manner.

Unless we learn to heed our negative emotions and our reactionary behaviours, they will become habitual, chronic and eventually disintegrate to levels unacceptable to ourselves and society. This way of living inhibits any freedom to live life to the full because we are ignorant of what could be; but creating an awareness of what could be allows the possibility of working with the very conditioning that initially caused these destructive emotions and behaviours.

It was my continuous feeling of lacking, or being 'less than', that drove me to desire, want and need to be. It was a continuous striving: my psychologist called it my 'drivenness' after success, power, relationships, etc. Having repeatedly achieved all of the above, I still found that after transient periods of feeling good, fulfilled or happy, I was again faced with a feeling of emptiness with the return of the added anxiety of what might happen rather than what was happening now. In my ignorance at the time, it was easier to continue with the familiarity of my fearful self (based on my past) rather than take the risk of surrendering to the unknown. I needed to be in control!

My misconception of self became a whole package of addiction in terms of my behaviour and appeared quite acceptable to society until the age of 45 years, when I spent the first of many stints in rehab. I was labelled a workaholic and an alcoholic, both of which deprived me of any spiritual cultivation. I may have been intellectually intelligent but was certainly deficient in emotional intelligence. I came from a family who already drank heavily, and I followed suit and medicated with alcohol socially in order to cope. While studying and working I excelled, which only justified my behaviour and perpetuated the entire addictive cycle. I gained degree after degree, travelled from country to country, had affairs and relationships, sold and bought properties like they were my last dinner, medicated with booze when anything felt uncomfortable and moved from what looked like one positive experience to another. Overall, I gained little or no ground, either physically, mentally, emotionally or financially. Each physical condition (the body), mental condition (the mind), emotional condition (the feeling), financial and social condition was slowly being eroded by my behaviour, which was becoming more and more addictive.

For me there was nothing better than to stand at the local pub on a Friday night and say, 'I've just been promoted' or 'I've just finished my PhD.' I would then have another drink, pick up the best-looking guy, have dinner and take him to bed with not so much as a second look the next morning. I was at the height of my addictive behaviour. Intermittent visits to rehab became the norm for me as the alcohol took a physical and psychological hold; on release I would return to the pub and repeat the behaviour. I was viewed as the returned war hero and forgiven by other addicts in the community and at my regular pub. My ego was still in control with strong internal feelings of pain and external emotional attachments still present.

This is only one example but there are many others, from minimal scapegoat behaviour such a shopping, to the extreme behaviour of terrorists and dictators. As Deepak Chopra said on *Larry King Live* in June 2009, 'Michael Jackson lived a mythical life and died a mythical death.' Perhaps his fearful perception of a 'not good enough' self played the last card and allowed his addiction to win. All are examples of addictive behaviours being 'acted out' due to our 'I' identification and self concept being threatened. These behaviours may be transient or become chronic and pathological and need both psychological and physical interventions.

Chronic addictions are often accepted by society as long as we do not appear to be inflicting too much harm to ourselves or others. As previously mentioned, my maternal grandmother, who lived to 97 years, was a chronic alcoholic who was always moderately inebriated but never appeared 'drunk'. Collapsing in public due to an excessive intake of alcohol or drugs, or attacking somebody, is unacceptable behaviour, whereas someone who is continuously busy, late, forgetful or even slightly inebriated appears quite acceptable.

Why do some people always appear to be so busy, forgetful or late? It may be genuine but more than often the 'busyness' is an escape from facing themselves in moments of complete solitude. For my current position in Saudi Arabia, I live in an expatriate compound in Riyadh. Over the weekends there is plenty of solitude due to a complete dearth of local outside entertainment, particularly for women. Many find it very difficult to remain on their own over the weekends and are always rushing around shopping, desert-walking or drinking gin and tonics at the Embassy, mostly to excess.

Forgetfulness can be due to being totally distracted by the movie inside our heads and subsequently being oblivious to external stimuli, which can sometimes lead to tragic consequences such as a child forgotten in a hot car.

Lateness is a form of superiority (the 'little me' concept) and creates the feeling of 'I am more important than you so you can wait', although there is always a valid excuse. A current example on a much larger scale is the American collective identity of self, which is now being threatened by a Middle East religious ideology, which itself also feels threatened. Here are two misconceived agendas facing each other, both ignorant of the fact that they are merely collective extremes of a wrong view trying to impose their view on each other.

We can see that if our actions and behaviours, for whatever reason, are contained in the limits of socially acceptable behaviour then we are not labelled and stigmatised with the terms 'alcoholic' or 'murderer' or 'sexual predator', etc. It is the end-point, a breaking point that has taken years of physical, mental, emotional and psychological conditioning to reach, that sees an individual's apparent self-destruction. Are we all so obsessed with obtaining possessions, money and technical velocity in order to achieve that we have become spiritually bereft and fail to notice or care until an individual or collective has reached a point of destructive behaviour harmful to us and/or themselves?

We now understand that addictions are not only the physical and/or psychological end-point of certain behaviours, but that the behaviours are stimulated by negative emotion. Where does this negative emotion come from? It comes from our negative mental thoughts, which not only afflict the mind but also create the accompanying emotion. Why and how do these negative thoughts arise? They arise from the sensory input that creates mental thoughts, coupled with memories based on our conditioned past, experience and genetics. It all takes place spontaneously via external stimulation and memory, imposing on our already misperceived self. This leads to unreal emotions that perpetuate reactive, compensatory and addictive behaviour. We tend to move from one unsatisfactory situation to the next in a repetitive cycle, which may feel like reality but is very unreal. Insanity has been said to be the repetition of the same bad behaviour over and over again with the expectation of a different result.

Misperception and misconception of self is a defect of the mind that creates unreal thinking and unreal emotions resulting in a deluded reality. This unreal thinking not only affects our own lives but the lives of others due to our constant needs, wants and demands, which cause both emotional and physical imbalances of mind and body. Hua-Ching Ni, the Taoist Master, sees the individual as a small universe creating energy that manifests both internally and externally, so the person can actually become heaven or hell. Society is invariably made up of individuals who are developing themselves in one direction or another so that heaven or hell can simply be the reality or non-reality of an individual's daily life.

As stated by Hua-Ching Ni in *Entering the Tao*:

People crave fame and profit and become bound by fame and profit. They crave wine and flesh and become bound by wine and flesh. They crave status and prestige and become bound by status and prestige. They crave children and grandchildren and become bound by children and grandchildren. They bind up the true nature in all sorts of mixed up ways, coming and going in the human world subject to unlimited suffering.

Our psychological sufferings based on all our ridiculous, confused thoughts can injure the physical body from within. When we view life through our imaginary self, our feelings of love and hatred can arise uncontrollably and cause us to further indulge our feelings with our addictive behaviours. Some individuals hold onto and hide behind rigid beliefs to protect their perception of self and are not aware that there is safety in 'letting go'. Wilfulness (the 'I' concept of self), as compared to willingness (surrendering to something greater than ourselves), is seen as the major obstacle to reality and is at the root of all addictions.

As individuals, we consciously regulate our behaviour and conduct to benefit ourselves. Addicts continue to benefit themselves even if it is damaging to their health and social status. The 'I' concept of self is so powerful that in the deluded belief, the gain of any good feeling from the addictive behaviour continues to outweigh any pain experienced from the addiction. How great is the harm of this wilful and misconceived self, not only to ourselves and others but to the world as we know it?

An ancient Taoist view, as outlined in the book *Taoist Meditation: Methods for Cultivating a Healthy Mind and Body* by Thomas Cleary, follows:

People's feelings have their particular blindness, a reason of which they cannot reach the 'way'. On the whole, this blindness is the subjective use of the intellect. When you are subjective, you cannot deliberately be responsive to events. When you use objective intellect, you can be spontaneous with clear awareness.

It is this blindness or ignorant sense of self that prevents us from viewing the world as it truly is and causes us to subjectively react and defend our deluded view of who we believe and feel we really are: our imaginary mind, created 'I' or mythical self. There are those who are spiritually responsible and are able to let go of their myth of self and surrender to a Higher Power. They have a willingness to accept what is because it 'already is'. They can also be religious but their religion is not who they are; they use it to assist them to live a moral, ethical and disciplined life. This is 'spiritual independence', the essence of the inner self, who you really are, and a life of reality.

In summary...

- Our perception of everyday events and situations is heavily influenced by our concept of self and how strongly we identify with our perceived 'I' or sense of self.

- We may intellectually rationalise that all is okay but still experience fearful and/or angry emotions due to a lack of awareness that a current situation has triggered an emotional past, which creates our concept of self.

- External circumstances are not the cause of our troubles. Our false sense of self, with its habitual and reactive thoughts, emotions and behaviours, is the cause of our suffering.

- This misperception of self creates unreal thinking and emotions resulting in a misperception of reality. The enjoyment of the moment is missed because our mind is always somewhere else, wrapped up in this misconceived self in an attempt to feel good.

Chapter 5

Breaking the cycle

ddiction can be thought of as being a cycle because it is a cycle of life that repeats and repeats itself *ad infinitum*, bringing more drama and misery into our lives. It is a cycle of suffering, or *samsara* as it is known in Buddhist philosophy. We are so busy living our illusion of self, so removed from reality living our own world of 'make-believe', that we miss real life and the enjoyment of the moment. Most of us are not aware that we are missing the meaning and fullness of our lives because we are so entrenched in our addictive behaviour.

We obsessively dwell on how we are going to maintain our deluded concept of self with all its aversions, attractions and addictive behaviours. Our personal sense of 'I' becomes totally identified with the misconception of self that it causes us to become driven, achieving more and doing more. The new property, new car or new job may temporarily create pleasant feelings, only to disperse with the return of feelings of emptiness and/or pain. Alternatively, some of us 'drop out' and do nothing except indulge our desires through drugs, alcohol and sex, remaining mentally, emotionally and physically vulnerable, thus repeating our cycle of suffering and being unable to feel truly alive. Some of us do both.

We incorrectly perceive and believe that our external circumstances are to blame for our current emotions of pain and anxiety; this is a deluded perception. The reason we genuinely feel that external circumstances are the cause of our suffering and addictive behaviour is that we have established this mythical view of self that continuously feels threatened, victimised or not validated by others. We therefore resist what 'already is' and remain in denial, unable to accept what is happening now, addiction and all. Our mind and emotional-identified self take over: 'This has happened before, poor me, I'm the victim, I'm being attacked.' We can attack back, invariably making the situation worse, or we can run away and deal with our emotions in private, invariably with compensatory and addictive behaviours.

With my predisposition for alcohol, family habits and conditioning, I chose to have a few drinks or even become drunk. Doing this shut off the mental chatterbox and eliminated any uncomfortable feelings. I medicated myself with alcohol. In my current employment as an eye specialist at a hospital in Saudi Arabia, with its very strict, conservative Muslim culture, I often feel angry at my lack of validation as a woman. My male peers and colleagues are not interested in my past, how many degrees I have, how qualified or experienced I am; I am employed to do a job and as a minority female in a majority male staff, I feel like I hardly exist. As a result, my ego can often feel a little bruised, but I understand that it has nothing to do with who I am but all to do with the Saudi male conditioning and culture. Perhaps I'm here for a reason; 'slaying of the ego' as it is called. While an alcoholic drink would flatten the mind and remove the feeling, it does not deal with the underlying emotion; it only temporarily suppresses it. I have now learned to deal with the situation by not personalising it and not allowing any unreal emotion to affect my wellbeing.

As Lama Yeshe said in his book *Introduction to Tantra: A Vision of Totality*:

> *Our constant search for peace of mind, security and happiness is based on a projection of ourselves which is not real so that we are living in a fictitious unreal world which is merely a projection of oneself.*

We all seek to escape our troubles, attempting to find some relief from the pressures of daily life. This may be in the form an addictive drug or some self-inflating activity that temporarily drowns the feeling of inadequacy or pain, physically and emotionally. There is an old tale of a rich man in India who gave money to a beggar in the street for no other reason other than to relieve his feelings of inadequacy and guilt for being rich and to gain a temporary good feeling. But all of these feelings are illusory.

As mentioned earlier, one of my previous and extremely enjoyable drinking companions (now deceased) was charming, delightful, witty and intelligent but also an alcoholic. I had seen him through many bouts of acute pancreatitis, which is known to be an extremely painful experience. Even so, he would reappear back in the pub no sooner than the episode had passed.

Some individuals with very strong wills find it humanly impossible to obtain insight into their behaviour, as quoted in the *Big Book* of AA:

There are such unfortunates. They are not at fault; they seem to have been born that way. They are naturally incapable of grasping and developing a manner of living which demands rigorous honesty. Their chances are less than average.

A less extreme form of addictive behaviour could well describe my mother, a highly intelligent woman who inadvertently dropped the seeds of acceptance of self and the psychology of Buddhism in my earliest and most formative years. Intellectually, she understood the concept of self but had no feeling or awareness that her own view of life could be tainted. Between her bouts of niceness, her prevailing emotion and behaviour was anger. She'd had an abusive childhood and an alcoholic mother, and this contaminated her present moment perception of self as being unworthy. She had a very strong will and ego of self-defence so that anything that was said or happened was seen as a threat to her illusory projection of self. This created constant confusing dialogue, which inevitably ended in arguments with family members or friends. It became a conditioned response of vengeance and scapegoat behaviour, triggered by feelings from her past. As I supported her during her final years, I had to remind myself that her changing moods were nothing to do with who I was. It has been said that when you think you are doing well at maintaining your emotional equilibrium, just visit your family for the weekend! My mother, who had a habit of provocatively imitating others, did so to me and it only registered much later. Emotionally it had passed right over me; I patted myself on the back.

The majority of us are driven by our addictive-thinking minds, experiencing feelings from unease, discontent, boredom or nervousness to more serious feelings of sheer panic or despair. This can be alleviated by addictive habits. Removing 'low key' unease can be quite enjoyable if the behaviour remains moderate, but if used to excess as in full-blown addiction, particularly with food, alcohol and drugs, sexual and criminal behaviour, the physiological and psychological tolerance increases. We require more and more of the addictive behaviour and/or substance to achieve the same feeling, which invariably is only a temporary and short-lived period of relief. We may feel we are only dealing with the psychological response, but for every addiction there is also a physiological component that affects the body's chemistry. Unfortunately, our addictions only compound the misery and drama already present in our lives. If we only remove the addictive substance and/or behaviour without any psychological support, we are left with a very deprived perception of self and a somewhat scary and painful reality, as well as possible withdrawal cravings. What do we do? Invariably we return to our addiction.

This unreal sense of self continuously intervenes in all experiences and creates unreal feelings. Unfortunately, the mind feeds feelings and feelings feed back to the mind; there is never a still moment of mind and/or feelings as they are in a closed-loop feedback system, which is an addiction itself. When feelings become too painful, it leads to physical behaviours to compensate for the pain. So as you can see we have an illusory thought, feeding an illusory feeling, feeding a physical habit or addiction, which then further compounds the feeling. The addiction of choice, whether it is sex, food, alcohol, heroin or criminal behaviour, may temporarily be mental heaven but is not reality. It merely repeats a cycle of suffering until intervention or eventual death.

This painful mind and emotion feedback system, temporarily relieved with our abusive habits, invariably has a pay-off or gain for us. As long as we feel the addictive habit is more pleasurable than our pain, we will continue to rationalise our addiction. We are deluded in our belief that our gain of pleasurable feelings from our addiction outweighs our miserable existence; for example, the pain of withdrawal symptoms from alcohol and drug addiction, or the pain of always being too fat or not thin enough, or the pain of having no intimate relationships.

When our physical and emotional pain begins to outweigh any pleasurable gain from our addiction, some of us reach a point of despair when we may decide to seek help or continue with the addiction until death. This moment of awareness or realisation can be triggered by a traumatic happening in an addict's life; for example, a car accident in which the driver had a high blood alcohol level and injured or even killed the passenger.

Families who cannot bear to watch their drug-addicted children any longer use intervention strategies and/or the now many rehabilitative counsellors who act as interventionists and assist families. These are the more severe cases that come to our attention, but there are also those who are still part of a family, who go to work and bring up children, who suffer day-to-day pain from an addiction or who are just generally pained at the lack of meaning in their lives.

To repeat an ancient Taoist proverb, as quoted in *Entering the Tao* by Hua-Ching Ni:

The superior man knows what should be known by him, the sick one does not know what should be known by him. And the one who is sick of being sick, therefore, can be free from being sick.

Our mind needs to become aware that it is the mind that has created the problem of this separate and misconceived identity of self. We therefore need to use the mind to dissolve this misconception of self, as it is this deluded view and feeling of who we think we are that is the origin of our addictive behaviour.

The degree and intensity to which we identify with our false view and belief of self is highly correlated to our compulsive and addictive thinking and behaviour, neither of which are real. We need to be able to escape from this mind-identified self, from where we derive our sense of self with its accompanying destructive emotions, leading to a false sense of pleasure and a false sense of pain.

When addictions become 'fully fledged' and damage the physical body, they become pathological and are labelled a disease. The gene or predisposition needs to be turned on or triggered, and it is our continuous negative emotions and behaviours which stem from continuous negative and addictive thinking that assist the process.

How do we begin to understand? How do we break this vicious cycle of destructive thinking and accompanying emotions that underpin our deluded view of self and lead to addictive behaviour? It is a willingness to change that acts like a catalyst in finding the truth of self, as well as an acceptance that we are powerless over our addiction; an acceptance that our life has become unmanageable; a willingness to surrender to a power greater than ourself; and the surrendering of our self will, giving up the deluded self that has always been in control.

As quoted in the *Big Book* of AA:

Free me from the bondage of self... a willingness, honesty and open mindedness are essential to recovery.

Many members of AA have said that they tapped an unsuspected inner resource that they identify as their own concept of a Higher Power, the essence of a spiritual experience, or for the more religious, a God consciousness.

Awakening to reality and a cessation of addictive habits needs continuous self-awareness and support, physiologically, mentally, emotionally and spiritually. This can be delivered through medical intervention in the case of substance abuse, but also needs psychological support via AA, counselling and/or a faith or doctrine; any one of life's philosophies and/or religions deliver a similar essence of moral and ethical living that help us find our truth. But as addicts we must not become our faith, thus confusing our concept of self with the ideology of our faith. This is not reality and can be decidedly limiting. Faith, belief and religion in essence support, direct and assist us to access who we really are, but strong belief systems can also be misconstrued as a deluded self and thus are no different from other harmful habits and addictions.

As you may have read in many books, changing your thinking changes your life, initially espoused by Deepak Chopra, one of the earlier well-known life coaches, in *Today's Wisdom*. This may be intellectually understood but it does not solve the basic problem of our destructive emotions that trigger our addiction.

As addicts, we need to be able to reduce or eliminate negative emotions and dissolve our false and deluded concept of self, conditioned by past experience.

We all experience negative emotions intermittently but that does not mean that all negativity is an inherent part of our nature, although research has shown that genetics do play a part. For example, most of us have heard of the happy newborn versus the continual screamer. Asian people tend to appear calmer than those from the west, which could be due to nature (genetics) or nurture (environmental conditioning) or a mixture of both. Genetics we cannot change but our perception and feelings of our conditioned past (nurture), we can.

This opens up the possibility of working with our conditioned emotions and the circumstances that initiate them. We need to develop an awareness of how we perceive and feel our sense of self in a given moment and how attached we are to this unreal concept of self.

As stated by Lama Yeshe in *Introduction to Tantra: A Vision of Totality*:

We must understand that we cannot manage our habitual concrete view of ego immediately but we can attack the grosser levels of misconception by loosening our tight grip on what we think reality is. All existent phenomena are mere appearances to the mind, lacking concrete self-existence. They come into being from an interplay of various causes and conditions, they arise, abide and disappear all the while constantly changing. This is true of ourselves as well, no matter what our innate sense of ego grasping believes, there is no solid inherent 'I' to be found.

It has often been stated that the addict is a seeker, although a misguided one, in a quest for pleasure. As Jungian psychologists espouse, addiction is nothing but a severely degraded substitute for the true experience of joy. Many addicts busy themselves seeking spiritual alternatives or answers, but these are all temporary attempts to alleviate their feelings of isolation and emptiness. Whatever the route we use for seeking spiritual fulfilment, whether religion, reading, praying or gurus, all are only facilitators to assist changing the misconception of self, or separate 'I', which masks the inner being of who we truly are. It is almost a matter of working backwards from our misconception of self to a perception of being one with ourselves and at one with others. We need to undo and erase the conditioning that has led us down the path of destruction. Only then can we access our inner essence and realisation of our true and real being. As stated by Dr Phil in his book *Self Matters*, we need to change our script and get rid of our fictitious self and discover our authentic self.

'Stay with the feelings, stay with the feelings,' resounded in my head during a rehabilitation group therapy session in Sydney. I used to think, as did the rest of the group, 'Is the counsellor mad?' I know now he couldn't have been more correct. At the time, it was much easier to jump back into my mind-identified self and think of something pleasant, such as meeting my friends at the pub, even though three weeks earlier I had been delivered to the rehab centre comatose from an excessive alcoholic binge. I had taken the wrong route to get in touch with my inner self by shutting down the mind with alcohol; at least I didn't shut down the whole body. As the psychologist spoke, all I heard repetitively was that the way to recovery was via my feelings: 'feeling is the healing' or 'healing is the feeling'. Feeling your way out of your addictive behaviour and addictive thinking is the only escape; it was the addictive thinking and behaviour that allowed me to escape from negative emotions and feelings in the first instance.

The following is a poem I wrote many years ago about the deluded emotions that accompany addictions:

How can this person begin to explain
Or rationalise behaviour that causes others pain.
The turbulent pathway of apparent self-destruction,
Incomprehensible to those of normal construction.

Wasted energy on the portrayal of I
One step ahead of the inevitable lie.
Experienced as real by the dysfunctional self
Bereft and void of any spiritual health.

Escaping reality and the avoidance of feeling,
The whirlwind of urgency that leaves others reeling.
Living the delusion of how I see me,
Instead of allowing those feelings just to be.

Insidious emotions that coil their way round
And prevent us standing secure on the ground.
Leaving us empty of a life of existence
Denying ourselves the serenity of acceptance.

At the height of our addiction, there are no real feelings. We may think we have feelings but these are illusory and unreal, invariably accompanied by physical feelings associated with the addiction or withdrawal from the addiction.

While completing a Masters degree in Rehabilitation Counselling specialising in drugs and alcohol and criminal rehabilitation, I was admitted to rehab for my own addiction. I escaped during a lunch hour to participate in a practical counselling exam at the university. I used all I had learned during group therapy session at the rehab centre the same morning. My examination subject was able to access her feelings and thanked me for the intervention, as she was experiencing a personal crisis in her life at the time. Unfortunately, I was unable to slow down sufficiently to contemplate my own feelings. I was still intellectualising the whole process, totally identifying my concept of self with complete lack of awareness as to why I experienced emotions that continued to drive me to drink.

A moment of epiphany, which I can relate to the beginning of my healing, came when a panic attack compounded by alcoholic withdrawal became totally overwhelming. I remember running down the stairs of my home to grab an ice pack out of the fridge as my heartbeat became louder and faster and I thought I was going to die. When that didn't work, I ran back up the stairs with a now faster heartbeat in search of a tranquiliser. At that point, I stood at the doorway of the bathroom and just said, 'Oh God, help me.' In those few seconds, I must have breathed a little more deeply. I became slightly distracted from my negative thoughts, which were only serving to compound my panic attack. My heartbeat was so loud and intense that I actually became aware of the beats slowing down.

That was the turning point for my panic attacks, which soon completely disappeared. I had allowed just enough gap in my stream of negative thoughts for something else to take over. The true essence of me, my being, Higher Power or God if you like, dealt with the situation once I got my mind-deluded egotistical self that wanted to be in control out of the way. My journey of awareness had already begun; some intervention was already taking place, whether you call it God or my true being beginning to manifest.

Now, every time I hit an emotional crisis I know to just stay with the feeling, breathe and 'let it be'. I just allow sufficient time for something else to take place. All I have to do is to surrender to what I am feeling, stay with the feeling without taking any action, and the feeling dissipates. It sounds simple but is not necessarily easy and takes many hours, weeks and years of mental discipline and practice.

So how do we intervene by dealing with an emotion such as anger before or after it arises? It is easier to reflect on an emotion after it arises, but that may be too late as you may have already dealt with the emotion, anger for example, via hateful words or behaviours toward someone or something, or obliterated any feelings with an addiction. You might later reflect on the damage done but this is more a reasoning or intellectualising of the behaviour, which may or may not assist you the next time you feel angry.

The thinking and arising of destructive emotions appear to us to be spontaneous and we often feel as though we have little or no control. Paul Ekman, a professor of psychology at the University of California and San Francisco Medical School, in discussion with the Dalai Lama in the book *Destructive Emotions: How Can We Overcome Them?*, suggests that we change our appraisals of what triggers our emotions and that will give us more time between the impulse to act on them and the actual reaction. The Dalai Lama also suggests that we need to cultivate a preparedness that allows us to instantly detect early signs of an emotion so we can prevent it from arising.

As addicts, obviously any substance abuse or abusive behaviour needs to be completely halted before we can even begin to work on any real awareness of a negative and/or destructive emotion, fed by our addictive thinking. We may also require medication to balance brain chemicals that have been damaged with a substance addiction. Some individuals have a dual diagnosis, for example an underlying psychiatric disorder, that can compound the triggers for addiction. Both conditions need to be medically treated in combination with psychological and self-awareness management. Only an holistic approach stands the chance of long-term success with addictions, particularly those that involve the addition of substance abuse.

Today I am a vigilant observer of my feelings and have the awareness and understanding as to why the feelings are present. I do not allow my mind to immediately attach and compound a feeling, at which point I would become the feeling and thus act out. I now stay with the feeling, even reflecting on it but not attaching to it, and not resisting it, just accepting the feeling however uncomfortable it may be. By staying with the feeling, it will eventually dissipate. Therefore, once an emotion or even a reaction to an emotion arises, do not analyse it with the mind, just feel it and accept it, stay with it and try not react to it.

Sometimes the feeling is just too overwhelming to contain and we may need to distract ourselves from it by doing something else. As an addict, the emotion may well have already moved on to a form of craving for the substance or behaviour previously used to alleviate the pain. An early favourite distraction of mine when in the middle of a full-blown panic attack was to extend and let go of an elastic band worn on my wrist, rather than dash for a alcoholic drink which I had previously done to relieve panic. A far safer method would be to go for a walk or reach out and talk to someone, rather than attack oneself, eat chocolate cake or swallow an alcoholic drink.

Focused breathing can be an instant distraction to any urge, craving or fearful emotion that may arise. By focussing on our breath, it returns our attention to the present moment; it brings us out of our mind and its associated emotions. Breathing and surrendering to the moment allows time for our inner essence or true being to take over. Bringing awareness to our breathing focuses our attention in the now and what is really happening, rather than acting on the story being played out in our heads. The only route to access our feelings is to totally surrender to them and not attempt to control them with our thinking, which only compounds the feeling and leads to an addictive urge and/or addictive response. You might ask, 'Surrender to what or whom?'. Surrender to what already is, let the feeling be by paying attention to the breath. This is true alert mindful awareness. Whenever you become aware of an overwhelming emotion or feeling, just focus instantly on your breathing. Focussed awareness of just one breath in and out is enough to begin the process, and with practice this can be expanded to minutes and even a mediative discipline for a set period each day.

With concerted practice of alert mindfulness and focussed breathing, my panic attacks disappeared, my craving for alcohol lessened and my fear of flying evaporated. When flying, I started thinking that I was already up there, thousands of feet above the planet, so why fight against what already was and partake in an alcoholic drink to eliminate my fear based on some imaginary concept of what might happen.

By getting in touch with inner feelings we can change what takes place on the outside because what we sense is happening externally is only a reflection of our inner mind and emotional turmoil. When I was breathing slowly, my heartbeat instantly slowed; I was allowing a gap for the universe to take over instead of my constant mental and emotional feedback based on my deluded conditioned beliefs and concept of me. The attention to breathing took me away from the destructive thinking which only served to compound the emotion already on board.

Perhaps you have already noticed when feeling angry that if you take time to contemplate your anger it appears to lose its strength. This momentary gap of awareness created by my distraction of breathing slowly and surrendering my mind-identified self was the beginning of my journey to reality and liberation. When I use the word 'liberation', I mean freedom from a mental and emotional bondage of self with all its addictive suffering. We need to feel inner emotions and stay with them to create a repeated awareness of any destructive emotions and their associated and conditioned thoughts that trigger these emotions. By removing our attention from the mind and its addictive thinking and feelings, we can create a space and allow this to happen. We remain aware but are not attached to the thoughts and accompanying emotions. It is only then that these illusory thoughts and feelings begin to weaken and dissipate, and reality thoughts and feelings are able to manifest.

Occasionally now I experience an habitual reaction, a feeling of unease or fear, or even a pleasurable sensation as a result of a situation, but I am aware that it is just a life situation and the feeling is not who I am. The feeling that manifests is an habitual feeling from my past and has very little to do with the present-moment circumstance. I know that in seconds or minutes the feeling will dissipate as long as I 'stay with the feeling' and just allow it to be. There is no need to identify with the feeling and allow it to become us and act on it. It is an unreal emotional memory from the past, triggered by similar conditions in the now. Letting go of the mind-identified self is a process or journey in reverse. We need to access our true being. Already in possession of an addictive nature, perhaps the addict will desire more 'being'?

In summary…

- The cycle of suffering continues as long we experience life through a false and unreal sense of self which creates unreal feelings. It becomes an emotional cyclic feedback system, temporarily relieved by our addictive habits.

- Moment-to-moment mindful awareness of our emotional state is the route to breaking the cycle of addictive thinking, feelings and habits. We need to stay with the feeling and not seek avoidance of the feeling by acting on it.

- Attention to our breathing distracts us from destructive thoughts and associated feelings. It allows a gap or space for any angry and fearful emotion to dissipate.

Chapter 6

Liberation

I cannot sufficiently emphasise the interplay between mind, thought and emotion and our resultant reactive behaviour, all of which are conditioned from the moment we are born. Half of the DNA in every cell in our bodies comes from each parent, and brings with it physical, mental and emotional characteristics. This is our blueprint for life before we even begin to think and feel. Our genes play a large part, and with each new life experience the interplay of mind, thought and emotion is conditioned, further compounding our false perception of self with its unreal emotions.

We will always find ways of escaping nasty or uncomfortable feelings, invariably based on our conditioned and ancestral coping skills. If your entire family took cocaine, it is more than likely that you will also use cocaine as an escape from your pain; if they were alcoholics, it is more than likely that you will use alcohol. Your genetic input, environmental conditioning and life experiences will influence the point at which you become a full-blown addict and your addiction begins to destroy you physically, mentally and emotionally. Personally, having been trolleyed almost unconscious with alcoholic poisoning into rehab God only knows how many times, the sheer physical and emotional pain forced me to change.

The first stage is to accept 'what is' because it already is; that is, we need surrender to our addiction, accept we have an addiction and then deal with the physical, emotional and mental experiences that trigger the addiction. It is necessary to be totally honest with ourselves and own our addiction rather than remain in a state of denial where everything external to us, such as family, friends and work colleagues, is screaming addiction. Acceptance that we have an addiction is the first and most important step in any of the recovery programs, whether it is a drug, alcohol, sex, food, gambling or other type of addiction, we need to admit that we have become powerless over the addiction and that our lives have become unmanageable.

The next step, as important as the first, is to be willing to get better, rather than allowing our deluded concept of self to be in control. We come to believe that a power greater than ourselves can restore us to sanity. Once we admit we have an addiction, we have taken the first step towards recovery. The first and most important move to clear thinking is self-awareness; awareness that it was our 'stinking thinking', as they call it in recovery programs, that created our misperception of self and resulted in our addictive behaviour.

Letting go of our misconception of self is where it begins. This principle is not new and has been supported by religions and cultures for centuries, but we don't have to believe in a Higher Power; all we need to do is become aware that our concept of self and accompanying emotions that underpin addictive behaviour are not real but an illusion. As quoted in the *Big Book* of AA, all twelve steps of any program are designed to kill the old false self and build a new free self, as it was the false self that stood in the way and ran us into addiction with all its shortcomings of hurts, bankruptcy, etc. With self-awareness, commitment and continued practice, our deluded self will begin to fade and our negative and addictive behaviour will begin to diminish. Self-awareness is meaningless unless we are committed to maintaining it and taking action to improve our addictive behaviour.

We need to break the grip of our deluded self and accompanying destructive emotions. It is very difficult to break our self concept, even a deluded one, as it is constantly reinforced by sensory input and emotional feedback of how I see 'me'. It is therefore easier to become aware of our destructive emotions either before or at least after they erupt, as I mentioned in the previous chapter.

The Dalai Lama calls this awareness 'mindfulness' and says that it can be used as a secular approach to cultivate awareness of our destructive emotions. These emotions feed back to the mind and compound our already skewed thinking, because we have identified and incorporated the emotion as part of how we perceive ourselves, invariably poor, unhappy me. Sheer disillusionment of an addicted, unhappy and separate me may break the bondage with our deluded self, but for others with perhaps a less intense unhappy self, continued awareness of emotions needs to be practised in order to break the bondage with the false self.

Now that you understand what is meant by a separate me or self, you will begin to appreciate why letting go of this false self is so important, particularly for the addict and especially when chemicals are used, which further distort the false image of self.

To summarise, when we interact with people or situations, we do so from our perception of me, so that we instantly judge or label the situation as good or bad, invariably based on our past conditioning and how it reflects our concept of self. This creates feelings of instant attraction or dislike of a person or object. Initially, it is easier to become aware of any feeling or emotion once it has arisen, but whenever this happens we need to make sure we create a moment or gap before taking action, thus allowing the intensity of the emotion to dissipate. With continued practised awareness, this process can become automatic during daily interactions with others and we become less inclined to overreact to any perceived emotion and/or situation. We also become less inclined to act on a strong urge to indulge our addictions, which we may later regret.

As we become more expert, we become acutely aware and are able to detect subtle signs of conditioned emotions arising. Mentally stepping back and creating a gap in our thinking in response to the emotion may preclude further compounding of the emotion with negative thoughts and behaviours. This allows the emotion to dissipate more quickly, thus quelling any urge for a reactive and/or compulsive and addictive response.

Eventually we can reach a level of awareness that we can break the link between the emotion and the initial sensory input, knowing that this is going to trigger a previously experienced negative emotion before any conditioned emotion has time to arise; any interaction with others will then be with us as people, our true selves, rather than through our separate and deluded concepts of self.

With concerted practice, we are able to eventually become mindful or aware of thoughts and emotional patterns that act as catalysts and trigger addictive behaviour. Finally, we realise that these trigger emotions are also unreal, based on our deluded thinking, conditioned by our very own choices and nurturing.

Certain situations and challenges will repeatedly trigger feelings and, being human, we will immediately interpret and relate these feelings to a painful past. This compounds our current feeling and so we experience a continual interplay of mind, thought and emotion, which Buddhism so aptly terms the 'cycle of suffering'.

Psychological counselling for addictions often analyses our past and makes us relive our past hurts, explaining that this is not who we are. It conditions a positive viewpoint in order to change the way we feel. This helps, but really just involves replacing a bad feeling with a good feeling, rather than letting go of the deluded self and connecting with who we truly are. We therefore remain hidden behind our delusional interplay of thought and feeling based on our past. Many people don't feel but instead just remain in their mental chatterbox from morning to night, continuously escaping from any feeling that might arise with some habitual and/or addictive behaviour; even the mental chatterbox can become an addiction.

An old Buddhist saying is, 'Never mind from whence the initial arrow came,' just remove the arrow and treat the wound. This means that we should accept what already is, the now, and be in the moment. In this moment, we are a smoker or a non-smoker, a food addict or non-food addict, an alcoholic or non-alcoholic. We cannot be both. We need to take responsibility for who we are and try not to defend it. Those of us who protest too much in defence of our condition, are our condition, such as the alcoholic pretending not be an alcoholic or the over-weight person pretending their weight is a family condition. This is denial: accept it and manage it.

We need to take responsibility for our condition. The initial responsibility is to pursue what has worked for others because we cannot eliminate an addiction on our own. One in twenty smokers who attempts to quit smoking on their own succeeds, whereas with community and medical help the number increases to twelve in twenty. Conditioned habits die hard due to our genetic input and life experiences. This conditioned, repetitive, mind and emotional feedback triggers the unreal mental emotional pain we feel and our addictions.

It is all very well to say we need to give up the behaviour that supports our addiction, but that really is only the very beginning. We need to be free of the emotion that triggers the addictive behaviour. How do we get there? We need to have alert awareness of our feelings and emotions as they arise. It's like a reverse cycle investigation when we return to the initial feeling and/or emotion so that the feeling becomes our journey to healing. We need to access whatever feeling arises, then feel it and stay with it. No feeling lasts more than 15 minutes before it changes to another; we cannot experience anger and happiness at the same time.

Being a complete addict myself, I notice that when I finish a meal or any pleasurable sensory experience I immediately want more. If I wait 15 minutes, the feeling dissipates and I no longer desire more. Addicts indulge the 'more than' syndrome or 'more than' feelings, which lead to 'more than' behaviours. Even when shopping, we buy three pairs of everything or never measure the amount of soap powder when washing, always using just a little more than it says to use on the packet.

As addicts, we need to maintain continuous moment-to-moment mindfulness, observing the thoughts that trigger the feelings when they arise and staying with the feelings rather than analysing them. Analysing our feelings will immediately connect our thoughts to the emotion, which then compounds the emotion by introducing memories of past experiences. This limits us to a cycle of addictive mind, emotion, feeling and behaviour. The answer is acceptance of 'what is'. Acceptance of our addiction is taking responsibility and reversing the 'cycle of suffering'. We do this via our feelings, being mindful of the presence of any feeling: alert mindfulness from moment to moment.

When Buddhist monks pray, they feel the prayer. Their display of movement and sound when chanting is useful in achieving the feeling. In all religions, meditation and prayer assist us in accessing our feelings, allowing any mind-made, imaginary thoughts and feelings to dissipate. This allows us to feel the essence of who we really are: just a person, a realisation of our true being. We are all expressions of life; it is our expression of being that allows us to live reality and not live our deluded self that controls and disrupts our lives.

Gregg Braden states in his book *The Isaiah Effect*:

Emotion may be considered the source of power that drives us forward towards our goals in life. It is the energy of our emotion that fuels our thoughts to make them real.

Alert mindfulness will assist in maintaining some form of reality from moment to moment, but if our thinking and emotions are deluded, and we allow this concept of a separate self to control our lives, we will move from drama to drama rather than from reality to reality in each moment of experience.

This is reflected in a statement from the Archbishop of Canterbury at the St Paul's Cathedral memorial service for the London bombings in July 2005: 'The individuals who carried out these perpetrations had their souls destroyed; they had no spirit; they had no reality.' I wouldn't say their souls had been destroyed, but they were living proof of an extreme deluded self based on a conditioned ideology with which they identified. This, coupled with fear, ignorance and a total lack of awareness of who they really were, led to an untimely death for both perpetrators and victims, and the above remark.

The easiest route to redefine what we experience on the outside is to address what we experience on the inside: our feelings, which are based on our thoughts and our body's response of emotion. Previously, we became our drama because we identified with it and needed crisis intervention to stop the cycle of repeated suffering. Bad habits take years of conditioning, as do good habits, such as the practice of moment-to-moment mindful awareness. We become the observer of what is taking place in our mind, its thoughts and accompanying emotions, not forgetting that this interplay of mind and emotion is also accompanied by physiological responses in the body. Little disciplines can be built on and changed in time just by the act of observing what is taking place physiologically, emotionally and mentally. Alert mindful awareness is the key to freedom from painful emotions!

Louise Hay said in the book *Today's Wisdom*:

We need to observe what is going on around us because invariably what is going on around us is a reflection of the feeling inside one, because from thoughts, feelings and emotions we create the conditions from within that we choose to witness on the outside. So don't beg the question why our bank account is empty, conditions at work aren't satisfactory and family members pick on you.

Our thoughts and feelings totally reflect how we view, think and feel our 'reality'. Our concept of self is created by our deluded thinking, feelings and reactionary behaviour, based on our memories and conditioning. We cannot be unhappy unless we have a story of unhappiness with which we identify and make our sense of self.

Vigilant awareness is the key: awareness of our emotions and reactionary behaviour to any feeling that may arise. Our moment-to-moment awareness or mindfulness will eventually allow us to understand that what we attract and experience in life mirrors our internal feelings in the moment. Haven't you observed that when you are feeling down, everything else during the day appears to go wrong? Nothing really goes wrong but the way we view situations, our attitude and behaviour reflect our inner feelings. The more in sync our feelings are with 'what is', the less reactive we will be. We will feel more comfortable and at ease with ourselves and not compensate our unreal feelings with obsessive cravings and addictive behaviour. By observing our thoughts and accessing our feelings, these unreal feelings based on our memories and past conditioning dissipate and we begin to live as a person with real feelings in response to life's real challenges.

Mindfulness or mindful awareness as a mode of treatment in health care has been introduced in stress reduction and reha- bilitation clinics in the USA and many other parts of the world. Although mindfulness has been viewed as a spiritual training, it can play a significant role in medical and psychological treat- ment programs. The medical use of mindful meditation has become increasingly popular, often eliminating and significantly reducing stress and managing chronic and terminal conditions. Mindful meditation emphasises accessing our feelings and dis-identifying from a false perception of self, a separate me through which we incorrectly view and live life.

We need to take the time to sit quietly in order to lessen the mental chatterbox and come out of the mind by feeling the breath. By focussing on breathing, we begin to breathe more slowly and lessen our attachment to our incessant thoughts. A small discipline of a few minutes each day can be expanded with practice. I accidentally took 10 seconds to lean against the door in the middle of a panic attack and suddenly became aware. My heartbeat slowed significantly and I continued to breathe deeply. This was a revelation. Today, the moment any feeling of agitation, anger or anxiety arises, I observe and become aware of the circumstance that triggered the feeling. I can react or just remain aware of the feeling and stay with the feeling until it dissipates. This doesn't mean I don't feel hurt or angry; I just stay with the emotion until it dissipates, even if it is intense. I am now able to trust this process from repeated practice and know that in minutes, hours or even a day I will feel calmer and differently about an emotional trigger situation. As we become more aware of our feelings, we become less reactive to life situations. We respond objectively to normal, everyday situations instead of having a subjective reactive response via the false self with a need to alleviate the resulting emotion. As stated by Jon Kabat-Zinn in *Wherever You Go, There You Are*:

> *It means you can stop taking yourself so damn seriously and get out from under the pressures of having the details of your personal life be central to the operating of the universe.*

When we stay with the feeling, we come right into the present moment and literally feel the feeling inside and stay with it. One of the easiest ways to slow the mind is to remain with the feeling and become aware of our breathing. The mind cannot focus on anything else while it focuses on breathing, and as we note and feel our breathing the emotions begin to lessen. For example, while I am preparing dinner a negative feeling of anxiety or resentment may arise. I am aware that the feeling does not belong to the present and is an emotion based on my past, triggered by my reflection on incidents from the day. I observe the thoughts and bring myself into the moment by feeling my breathing and concentrating on chopping the vegetables rather than chopping off my finger because I am stuck in a thought pattern attached to an emotion. Previously, I would have pre-empted the feeling by having a drink, and then gone into judgemental mode about everyone else who was at fault during the day and had offended my false self, rationalising a second and third drink to quell any uncomfortable emotion.

Slowly, feelings fade from each experience and we can continue comfortably until the next thought and emotion arise. We can apply the same breathing technique until the feeling dissipates. An example of this is when I go to the bank and sensations of anxiety and nervousness manifest based on my past financial insecurity and fears. It feels very real, so I observe and do not analyse, and concentrate on the present moment activity. I no longer allow past emotions to contaminate my now. An extreme example is the true story of a Chinese passenger on an airliner about to crash into the mountains. Totally accepting his impending death, he collected his briefcase and wrote of his love to his family with the hope that the letter would be found. I doubt that many of the other passengers were able to achieve the same in their moment of extreme fear.

Remaining constantly aware of changing bodily sensations and feelings, staying with the feelings and concentrating on breathing will allow release of unreal emotions, which in turn will become less frequent. We may ask, 'How can I do all this while doing something else?' From real experience, it is possible! For example, I might be in my consulting room examining a patient and I will hear my reactive mind saying, 'I wish this kid would look at the fixation target and his father would cease interfering'. I am aware that this is a reactive thought in response to my judgement of another's unacceptable behaviour, which has nothing to do with my current act of examining the patient. If we attach to the thought and feelings instead of allowing them to just be, we will allow them to contaminate the present moment and they may eventuate into a confrontation.

A rehab counsellor for addictions was asked, 'What is the essence of these rehabilitation programs?' He just drew a big 'I' and a smaller 'I' next to it. That was his answer, which indicated reducing and eliminating the false perception of 'I' and becoming just the person I am. The ego is based on our deluded concept of self, which feeds the illusory feelings, which feed back to the mind and further compound our cycle of suffering and addiction. Mindful awareness assists in reversing this cycle until the bondage with our mythical self of false concepts and feelings is broken and we begin to live reality.

Behavioural medicine has already proved that by working on mindful, moment-to-moment awareness, anger, which can lead to anxiety headaches, hypertension, allergies and unhealthy habits such as addictions, can be lessened and/or eliminated. The process of mindfulness can be translated as the depersonalising of the feeling of 'I'. The more we analyse our feelings, the more subjectivity and 'I' will be present, which only compounds conditioned feelings and addictive behaviour. This causes feelings of separation and internal loneliness regardless of how many material externals, successes and friendships we appear to have accumulated.

We cannot stop our thoughts but do not need to become entangled in them; that is, do not analyse them, just be an observer of them. An analogy is passing clouds: view the cloud prior to passing, not wondering what shape it is or where it is going. In the same way, observe your thoughts, not attaching to them, as they may be based on past guilt or future insecurity. We remain mindful and totally aware in the moment of passing thoughts, feelings and emotions. The idea is to stay with the emotion, not rush out and try to alleviate it by jumping through hoops, having a heroin hit or yelling at somebody else. Stay with the feeling and the feeling will dissipate just like the clouds.

To summarise, the only way to reverse this cycle is to stay with the initial feeling and it will dissipate. Through alert moment-to-moment mindfulness, emotions and feelings are neutralised, dissipating emotional and mental states with all their attached dramas. Awareness is becoming aware of the thoughts that trigger the feelings, the feelings that trigger the cyclic pattern of suffering supporting and maintaining the separate and false self that underpins addictive behaviour.

When you hear the word 'emptiness' in the Buddhist philosophy of living, it really means emptying the mind of addictive thinking and associated addictive and destructive emotions and feelings.

A Zen Buddhist saying, as quoted in *The Great Awakening* by Robert Powell is:

Only when you have no thing in the mind and no mind in things, are you vacant and spiritual, empty and marvellous.

The Zen experience of enlightenment is really going from emptiness to reality, emptying ourselves of our mythically perceived self, a deluded self that triggers unreal feelings based on painful memories and a fearful future. Letting go of our past and our projected future does not mean forgetting knowledge, professional and life responsibilities. It means letting go of past perceptions and concepts, those conditioned concepts that created the feeling of me, our deluded feeling of false security that conceals our pain, doubts and fears and acts as a catalyst for our addictive behaviour. Life can be just as hectic as before, but with a difference: there is no personal deluded 'I' or myth of self involved, our 'I' therefore lives reality.

Once we realise and become aware of the unreality of our thoughts and feelings, which are forever looking for ways to bolster the false self by attaching to physical, mental, emotional and even spiritual gain, we surrender to the process of 'just being' by accepting 'what is' because it 'already is'. It is only then that we will be able to feel those perfect moments without our fix. We need to dis-identify from the mind, with all its devious calculations, to preserve the false 'I' and not allow the present to be mentally and emotionally contaminated by past or future fears.

The mind is used in many activities such as applying for a job, driving the car, paying the bills, etc., but should not to be wasted on hours of rationalising and reliving past experiences and emotions that lead to the return of habitual and addictive behaviours. Letting go of the bondage of self lessens destructive emotions and thus addictive behaviour, which eventually weakens with continued practice of moment-to-moment mindful awareness.

We know how outside events can trigger our minds and emotions to run amok, and we rush to escape the painful feelings, hence the word 'mindfulness.' Moment-to-moment mindfulness is a sense of awareness in which we become conscious of every moment in the now. It is difficult, but with time and practice we can begin to recognise and feel the unreal self that contaminates the now with thoughts and feelings that belong to the past or future. Mindful awareness allows us to break away from unreal thoughts and feelings and return to reality. Only our conscious awareness is present and we become that presence by just being. We become conscious of being conscious.

Old unreal feelings will re-emerge from time to time. Being aware of any bad feelings, particularly when we are not stressed, is an indication of how much false me is still present. These unreal emotions can suddenly erupt in a quiet moment so that we need to reflect on our inner comfort, as it is an excellent measure of where we stand on our journey to reality. Initially, real moments of peace may only be fleeting but we can become aware of which feelings are real and which are unreal, which are good and which are bad. Reality good feelings will increase in time without external validation, material objects or substances to make us feel good. Moments of that tipsy champagne feeling will slowly infiltrate our daily life, even without the champagne!

The more time we spend on mindful awareness of how we feel, the more the unreal emotions will manifest and dissipate, and we will reach a point of comfortable being. When challenges do arise, we will act objectively in contrast to living our imaginary and deluded self with its very subjective, defensive and reactive behaviour. The Buddhist practice of 'bare attention', or moment-to-moment mindful awareness, or just mindfulness, are all used to quieten the mind. Our thoughts or attention are then without judgement and totally accepting of what already is. We may not be happy with a family member or work-related situation for example, but judgement only introduces past toxic thoughts and emotions with resultant habitual and reactive behaviours. It is only a life situation, it is not who we are unless we identify with it.

The following Serenity Prayer, originally by Reinhold Niebuhr and adopted by AA and other twelve-step programs, is simple but summarises it well:

God, grant me the serenity
To accept the things I cannot change;
Courage to change the things I can;
And wisdom to know the difference.

Eventually, the ego relaxes and we reach a state of mental calmness. The Taoism term 'wu-wei' (non-interference), the Zen Buddhism saying 'Surrender to the nature of things', the Christian saying 'Surrender to the will of God' and the Islamic saying 'Surrender to the will of Allah' are all similar. This awareness stills the mind so that we are passive but alert to act, but not react with habitual and addictive behaviour. Living a life of wu-wei or alert awareness brings mental tranquillity and reality and acceptance of the nature of things, instead of an agitated search for more excitement, physically, mentally and emotionally.

We can now see that freedom from the false self arises from taming the thoughts and emotions that attach to the untamed mind. I use my mind or my memory but I do not allow my mind or memory to use me; the mind can be our freedom or our prison or 'shackle'.

As the poet William Blake said:

In every cry of every man, in every infant's cry of fear, in every voice in every man, the mind-forged manacles I hear.

We now understand that our mind-made addictive thinking compounds our unreal emotions that lead to unnecessary addictive behaviour. Reality living, therefore, is not only freedom from our physical addictions but freedom from our unreal mental, emotional and physical suffering, and therefore our addictions.

In summary…

- Letting go of the deluded self is where liberation from our addiction begins. Committed practice of mindful awareness of destructive emotions as they arise is the route to freedom.

- We will eventually become aware of emotional patterns that trigger addictive habits and be able to take personal responsibility in that moment not to follow through or act on any craving and/or desires.

- We become the observer of what is taking place within, mentally, physically and emotionally. Little disciplines of mindful awareness can be built upon until we become the observer of the emotions and not the emotion.

Chapter 7

Reality living

Imagine feeling contented and peaceful with a knowing feeling that all is okay whatever the circumstances, and not being dependent on continuous external stimulation in order to feel good. We can still enjoy the good feeling of a new house, car, promotion at work and relationships but still remain aware that these are only temporary situations, and our inner essence and feeling of who we are must not be dependent on what's 'out there'.

Our driven and constant search for achievement, security and material gain, compounded by today's media of what we should be and what we should buy, does little to assist us in realising that it is not who we need to be or who we are. We excel at what we do, good or bad, individually and collectively, to justify and bolster our feeling of a secure self. We exhaust ourselves with our constant judgements and plans to support the existence of 'I'. We tear down somebody else's 'I' in order to make our own 'I' feel better or alleviate our feelings of a hurt self worth with our addictive behaviour. Any addiction is the means to an end of substantiating the existence or security of 'I'. It is a very deluded means to an end. Examples include: the person suffering from anorexia who feels totally in control of an unreal view of their body; the alcoholic quelling the hyper-active mind and/or feelings of fear; the dictator enhancing the existence of 'I'; an undemocratic government reflecting the collective existence of 'I'.

An individual who performs heinous acts is no different from a heroin addict; they are both in pain and suffering from despair, which they can't bear to feel. An extreme existence of 'I' is reflected in acts of terrorism or violent crime, which the individuals feel are justified by their beliefs. They have no feelings for their victims' suffering; they can't even feel their own suffering because they are so out of touch with who they are and with reality. Queen Nor of Jordan stated on *Larry King Live* in August 2005, 'These people live in a fantasy world which is not reality. Their self-esteem is zero, they became someone, even if an evil someone, only to be annihilated by their false ego.' As mentioned in *Destructive Emotions*, it is the Dalai Lama's belief that some individuals neglect human compassion and simply concentrate on the brain to the exclusion of all else, thus losing balance and only viewing life through their deluded, psychological self. It is then that disasters and unwelcome happenings occur in their lives.

The most important feeling of an internal contentment, not dependent on external stimuli, can only be obtained and maintained by a still or quiet mind. We have to employ the mind to get back to reality to live a life of contented sobriety. I like the Chinese term 'wu wei' meaning 'effortless purpose', as it implies a heightened state of awareness with a minimum of doing. We need not seek spirituality; it will come to us when our outer world begins to reflect our contented inner world regardless of what is happening around us. The mechanics of family, friends and work take care of themselves.

Krishnamurti said, as quoted in *The Great Awakening*:

The man who is liberated himself no longer has any desire to 'be'.

We need to live entirely in the present of the eternal now, which is reality. Living our psychological self, conditioned by the past and fear of the future only exists in our imagination; the past recreates itself as memory with which the self identifies and our future then becomes our past. Death of the psychological and false self is a requirement of reality.

An enlightened or liberated person lives reality, and lives life as a person and not through their deluded concept of self. They are a person doer, not a perceived doer, just taking action on what needs to be done rather than living in a state of continuous reaction to what already is. If everything we accomplish is from a judgemental and defensive mode, then we are again living our past and unreality. We move into our mythical self of deception and fantasy and move away from our true being. We can still have initiative, be successful and even experience adversity but need not make the experience our identity. We need to become aware that everything in this world is temporary; nothing is permanent although we try very hard to make everything so. Conflict will always arrive when we insist that situations or things have to be. It is then that we become unhinged due to our susceptibility to destructive emotions and resulting addictive behaviours.

To date, we have misinterpreted our deluded thoughts and feelings to be our existence; our perception of 'me' or 'I', the 'mythical self' that creates a feeling of separateness from others with a continuous desire 'to be'. The greatest cost of living our mythical self, which is deceptive and not real, is the loss of intimacy. We are never close to others or feel at ease with others because we perceive any experience and our perceived self as separate. We do not feel as if we belong. If we wish to connect with others and truly feel liberated then we need to be liberated from our mental shackle of the deluded self.

Observe the people with whom you currently share your life; they will invariably reflect your degree of liberation. Some people reside totally in their deluded, mind-identified self with its driven and addictive thinking and behaviour; they are never in touch with their feelings and wonder why their lives consist of crisis after crisis. If you have drama in your life it is a reflection of what is going on inside your head. It is this lack of awareness that perpetuates this repetitive cycle of a deluded mind and unreal feelings, leading to reactive and addictive behaviour. The cycle needs to be broken and reversed.

So how do we maintain this state of being that leads to reality living with contentment? We need to reach and maintain a state of equilibrium which is less vulnerable to life's changing conditions and challenges. Moment-to-moment mindfulness is a continuous awareness of what is actually happening with one's thoughts and emotions and behaviours. Initially it may only be an awareness that our thoughts and feelings are mostly based on the past, our mental baggage. Continuous mindful awareness keeps us in touch with any feeling that may arise and an alert observer of the thoughts associated with the feeling.

As stated by Krishnamurti in *The Great Awakening*:

It is the immediate perception of truth that is liberating, not ideation. Ideas merely breed further ideas. And ideas are not in any way going to give happiness to man. Only when ideation ceases is there being, and being is the solution.

Mindful awareness can therefore be viewed as a secular discipline that allows us some control over our thoughts, otherwise our thoughts and emotions tend to be controlled by our reactive impulses, leading to addictive behaviours. Long-term transformation can only come about through the process of mental discipline and meditative training so that our emotions are a reflection of an inner reality rather than a reaction to imposed outside events. We need to maintain an inner calmness and develop compassion, kindness and equanimity; true inner happiness can only arise from these virtues. It is only when we have eliminated the deluded false self, with all its talk of judgement, doubt, analysis and confusing verbal garbage going nowhere, that the mind begins to function in a reality framework that can then lead to mental peace and contented feelings.

Awareness of our breathing can alert us to any feeling of anxiety or fear, as our breathing changes with any feelings of stress. Focussed breathing can be practised as a meditative discipline by concentrating on our breathing for as little as five minutes each day, expanding the time with practice. Eventually the discipline can be introduced into every moment of daily living. For example, if we encounter a stressful situation, we just need to breathe and let the feeling be, and if possible continue with whatever we are doing. We need to just observe the emotion and associated thoughts and not get tangled up in them, analyse them or instantly act on them. Instead we need to allow a gap. In just moments, the excess anxiety will dissipate and we are able to respond more rationally to the stressful situation.

It sounds like an impossible task, but with practice and effort we can create change in the way we feel, think and behave. Moment-to-moment mindfulness can become part of our very being so that in every situation we are present as a conscious being without any preconceived judgements about anything or anyone. Without judgement, there is nothing to forgive because, in effect, we have already forgiven the moment by accepting what already is. We should not respond personally to another person's bad behaviour because it has triggered our painful past. We need to give up our emotional memory, give up the 'I' as the centre of the universe, the 'me/mine' feeling of what we think is reality. It is this psychological attachment to a conditioned memory that creates our deluded feeling of happiness inevitably to be replaced by our dcluded feeling of unhappiness.

In every waking moment there are aspects of our lives that we may like or dislike, and there may even be adversity, but they don't need to represent who we think and feel we are. As Iyanla Vanzant, author, counsellor and friend of Oprah Winfrey, announced on *The Oprah Show* in May 2007, 'You either got it or you ain't got it.' She was alluding to the feeling of reality, a life of mental and emotional freedom.

In summary, the following points will assist:

- Remain vigilant with moment-to moment-mindful awareness of thoughts, feelings and behaviours.
- Stay with any feeling as it arises. Do not react immediately or act on the feeling or try to suppress any feelings of anxiety, fear or hurt.
- Do not analyse or mentally attach to negative thoughts and feelings as they arise.
- Allow the gap of thought and feeling to just be; just be the observer and accept the moment.

It is the gap of thought and emotion not acted on that is so important. By allowing it just to be, without reaction, allows the emotion that triggers the addictive craving and/or behaviour to dissipate. For example, now I don't have to wait 15 minutes for my desire for more to go away; the feeling dissipates in seconds, even though my addictive mind might still be in the habit of thinking 'why not?'.

With repeated practice and time, the gap becomes part of us, then becomes us: our conscious being from moment to moment. Our conscious being becomes an effortless purpose; the experience and us are one. We don't need to procrastinate about anything due to fear, as it all becomes part of 'what is' and we become part of 'what is'. When there is no separate sense of self, there is true liberation, a 'surrendered reality', free from our mental prison of a conditioned past. When we completely let go of our false self, the ego dies and allows our true being to manifest, the essence of who we truly are. We are able to let go of our conditioned addictive temperament and its self-destructive behaviour.

The practice of mindful awareness is a responsible discipline of our emotions, and results can be measured by the degree of peace that we encounter. Moment-to-moment mindfulness still uses the mind, but not the agitated, reactive mind with its associated negative feelings and addictive behaviours. It is the realisation or feeling of our own conscious presence that allows for comfort when alone and with others, or even just stability when bad things happen. It allows our inherent qualities of humility and compassion to manifest. This means we can be free from an addictive mind and addictive experiences and behaviours. But to reiterate, the ego or deluded self loves to take control and will seize any opportunity to reinforce itself by identifying with our fears, especially when under pressure rather than facing the pain that lives in us. For example, in our relationships 'spider love' is not real love but instead a control love where we attack or spite the other person to make ourselves feel better. But we think we love them! It is only a myth of a good feeling or a myth of a bad feeling.

Paula Abdul, a judge on *American Idol*, stated on *Larry King Live* in May 2006, 'Anorexia is always with you. It's not about the food; that's just the behaviour. It's all about the feeling.' Personally, I think alcoholism is always with you. It is not about the alcohol, it is about the feelings we experience. We need contented feelings to experience contented sobriety. We have to learn that feelings are the clue. Feelings are the window to healing and to letting go of a destructive and addictive self. We can't just fix the mind and we can't just fix the feeling, as we attempt to do with our diversions and medications. We have to feel the feeling, stay with the feeling and work through the feeling. We use the mind to do this, but again we shouldn't let the mind use us. The only escape from our unconscious, compulsive and addictive thoughts, emotions and behaviour is to access our feelings and literally feel them. Only then are we *en route* to being in touch with our true self and reality.

Once we realise this superficial and false self, accompanied by unreal feelings, is the source of our addictive behaviour, we will become aware that there is a real or true self. Once we start to own or accept our feelings of fear, anger and resentment and work with them, we find they lessen and dissipate more quickly. By taking responsibility for our feelings, we begin the journey to emotional freedom. We then begin to realise that our perception of external conditions is only a reflection of our feelings within. The more we judge and resist the present moment and the more we ignore our feelings, the more our addictions will prevail. Our life's difficulties are only a reflection of our mental and emotional state of resistance to the present moment of what already is.

As Louise Hay said in *Today's Wisdom*:

Look at your life, your relationships, your friendships, your bank balance, and external circumstances. They will all reflect what is going on inside you because your view of life, based on your feelings within, will eventually play out.

Yes, bad situations occur, such as loss of a relationship, loss of a home, or loss of money. These are life situations but they are not who we are. We need to accept and acknowledge that life can be difficult and extremely challenging at times, and it is only by accepting and surrendering to the painful feelings experienced due to a particular life situation that we can actively face our challenges. As M. Scott Peck stated in the opening chapter of his book *The Road Less Traveled*:

Life is difficult but once you realise it is difficult you will find life easy.

Therefore, surrender to 'what is' because it already is; it has already happened, good or bad. There is nothing wrong with setting goals and striving to achieve; the mistake is substituting any success or failure experienced for our feeling of self, so that when we fail we become the failure. These are purely life circumstances and experiences and not who we are.

We should not misinterpret the word 'surrender'. Surrender means letting go of our inner resistance to what already is. It means we should resist making judgements of what is happening in the present moment, based on an interpretation made by our false self. During my addictive past, I would judge each and every situation with all the emotional negative feelings attached, which would then give me justification to have as many drinks as I wanted after work because I'd had a 'bad day'. The denial of our addictive behaviour becomes the addictive self. Some of us replace one addiction with another addiction, but the pain and suffering due to resistance of 'what is' will continue with non-acceptance of the problem. Some of us might say, 'I'm glad I am a heroin addict' or 'I'm glad I am an alcoholic.' It was a wake-up call to some of us that we were living a mind-identified life of sheer hell, very far removed from the truth of who we really are and reality.

To summarise, our deluded self is highly correlated to the intensity of any reactive feelings and behaviours we might display, triggering false feelings and addictive behaviours that in time become our addiction. We need to surrender to what life offers rather than opposing life. We should surrender to 'what is' and learn to take responsible action in the moment rather than a defensive reaction based on unreal feelings. Not surrendering to 'what is' supports the deluded self and creates a separate sense of self out of sync with ourself, others and reality. This selfish behaviour, particularly the addictive type, lacks both empathy and compassion, viewed daily in communal and individual social behaviour. We are all responsible.

The Chinese Taoist philosophy of 'wu-wei', of not interfering with the course of events, not acting against what is thus coming back to the point of surrender and surrendering to the moment, is taking responsibility in that moment. For example, I needed to accept that I had the disease of alcoholism and surrender to the fact that I am an alcoholic regardless of the precursors of how I became an alcoholic. Surrendering to my alcoholism did not transform the alcoholism, it transformed me.

I have to laugh as I regale the story of a close girlfriend who wasn't an alcoholic but was having relationship problems with her husband and family. Attending one of my AA meetings where a female recovering alcoholic who had been in the program for many years was speaking, my girlfriend suddenly said, 'Oh, now I get it, I'm the problem!' That was the start of her liberation, the spontaneous realisation that her interpretation of things was wrong.

Eventually I became aware that I attended AA meetings for the feeling: it was like a 'psychological injection' or a 'free psychology class' where I was able to empty myself of deluded thoughts and feelings and leave with a good feeling of just being myself.

Initially at AA meetings we may not connect with our feelings, but attend purely for control input. This is still better than risking death from our addiction. We might try to stop our addiction by, for example, stopping sex, stopping eating, stopping drugs, or stopping drinking. This is purely control and the pain will always be present, compounded by the desire to compensate the pain with another hit of heroin or a drinking binge. The risk of 'busting' is extremely high because we have not accessed our feelings. A good analogy, recently reported on a Saudi television program, stated that 'Ramadan Muslims' or 'Christmas Christians' were only Christians or Muslims on special days and did not connect with the essence of their religions during the rest of the year. Regular attendance at AA meetings, whatever the addiction, and time with psychological support from counsellors and family, usually allows us to access our feelings, leading to real recovery.

Habitual escape from our feelings through addictive behaviours only compounds the situation, and more and more escape routes are needed as tolerance develops with obvious repercussions. The only way through is a realisation, to which many a recovered addict will attest. It is only through awareness of our feelings that we will taste liberation from destructive emotions. We need to surrender to our feelings, because feelings are the route to healing our addiction. It is the only access to our true being and the essence of who we truly are. Our quality of life has a different, more vibrant energy with an inner knowingness, which connects with other people's inner and equal energies. Our entire work, relationship and life ethic changes as we connect with our inner being and the being of others of a similar vibration.

Eckhart Tolle ends his book *The Power of Now* with a quote:

> *You surrender the past powerless when you realise that nothing you ever did or was ever done to you can touch the true essence of who you are.*

It is our true being which is the answer. It has always been present and will always be present, hence the words 'eternal' and 'eternity'. Celebrating the year 2000 in Australia, the Sydney Harbour Bridge lit up the word 'Eternity'. This represented the title of a book written about a recovering alcoholic who chalked the word 'Eternity' on Sydney pavements; that was his expression of his inner essence of eternal being.

In summary...

- Alert mindfulness becomes our key to freedom and reality living. By observing our thoughts and accessing our feelings, unreal feelings based on a conditioned past will dissipate and we will begin to live the person, with real feelings in response to real challenges.

- We begin to respond objectively to normal everyday situations instead of subjectively via a false sense of self with the need to alleviate the resulting emotions. We surrender to the process of just being, letting go of our inner resistance of what is by accepting what already is.

- Once we are aware that the false sense of self with unreal emotions is the source of our addiction, we will be aware of a true or real sense of self, the person in touch with reality and reality living.

Conclusion

The heroin addict taking his hit, or the terrorist who has just blown up himself and others are both examples of people's deluded attempts to make themselves feel good. Unfortunately, this insane behaviour creates chaos, pain and suffering in other people's lives, as well as their own if they remain alive. What they don't realise is that in their attempt to feel good, they are already feeling so bad that they are in a living hell. Why? They are incorrectly identifying their life circumstances with their already conditioned and misconceived negative perception of self with all its associated emotional suffering. Their route to feeling good is back-to-front, based on a delusional concept of 'I'. This mythical 'I' remains separate, in control, superior, intolerant of others and invariably threatened by others. Whatever the route used to gain that mythical good feeling, it is based on a conditioned, physical, mental and emotional past. When addictive behaviours and substances are added to the mix in order to bolster the feeling of 'me' or remove painful feelings, the cycle of suffering is compounded. Unfortunately some seek death to escape emotions that are too painful to face mentally and emotionally.

A quote from Eckhart Tolle's book *Stillness Speaks* summarises it beautifully:

All the misery on the planet arises due to a personalised sense of me... a mind-made self as a substitute for your beautiful divine being... that false sense of self then becomes your primary motivating force.

Freedom from our deluded self and accompanying destructive emotions and addictive behaviour can only be obtained by continuous mindful awareness: a vigilant awareness of any emotions as they arise. The technique could be described as a gym for emotional education and training. By staying with the emotion, we remain in the moment and are already taking responsibility for any potentially destructive emotions, by delaying the emotion which could lead to a reactive and/or addictive behaviour. It is a mind–body intervention. With practice, we are able to release any potentially destructive emotions such as grievances, resentments, self-pity and anger, which not only contaminate the present but act as triggers for our addictions.

Once we become aware of these destructive emotions and how they affect ourselves and others, we can work vigilantly on our mental antidote. Medication may be needed to assist the brain's chemical balance, preferably not long term, although if there is an underlying psychiatric disorder there may be a case for long-term drug medication. Psychological counselling certainly assists but we must not remain dependent on continuous outside help. Mindful awareness practice places the responsibility completely in the hands of the addict, where we like to be 'in control'.

Meditation is a form of mindful awareness that takes time to practise but is known to calm the mind and create a calmer disposition. It has also been shown to have physical effects on the body's stress response of lowered levels of cortisol, high blood pressure and chronic conditions such as headaches and painful joints. But can continuous mindful awareness ultimately and completely free us of our deluded psychological self and thus our addictive behaviour? It can, by training the mind to be alert to our emotions as they arise, allowing the gap before the emotion becomes destructive, thus triggering addictive behaviours.

We go though a kind of emotional death as we come to terms with our addictions, similar to those facing impending death, as described by Kübler-Ross in the book *Further Along the Road*

Less Traveled by M. Scott Peck. We pass through emotional releasing stages towards our psychological growth: first there is denial of our addiction; next are feelings of anger that we have to change our thinking; then there is bargaining with the truth of the situation; depression often comes next once we begin embrace the reality of the situation; and finally, we reach a stage of acceptance of our addictions.

By acting on our emotions through contemplative mindful awareness, we are able to change our thoughts, emotions and moods, thus allowing a more stabilised temperament and more ability to cope with daily life, eventually learning to like what we are required to do. Mindful awareness meditation trains us to observe our thoughts and feelings without reactivity. This simple mental training of mindful awareness helps people in all walks of life cope on a daily basis. As a recovering alcoholic was heard to say, 'God willing, we never have to deal with drinking again but we have to learn to deal with sobriety, our quickness to anger and our sensitivity to criticism, and above all reject the fantasy of our deluded self and accept reality.'

Freedom from emotional pain and freedom from addiction can only take place when we begin to realise our inner essence of being, who we truly are, which up until this point has been obscured by a fantasy life created by a deluded perception of self. Just being, and not living our mythical separate self, allows us to develop equanimity and perceive ourselves as part of the world, equal and the same as everyone else. With time, we become very aware of how our previous behaviour affected others and begin to develop feelings of empathy, compassion and kindness so that our being becomes empathy, compassion and kindness with an awareness of these attributes in others. When we experience unacceptable behaviour from others, we will no longer take it as a personal affront; we become aware that the bad behaviour belongs to them. We don't identify our perception of self with the situation in which we find ourselves. We need to be aware that the other person is in pain for whatever reason and not judge them; they are suffering, as once we were, and have their own journey to travel. This allows for forgiveness of unacceptable behaviour and pre-empts a defensive reaction as reflected in the saying 'God forgive them because they know not what they do'.

A quote from the book *A Course in Miracles*:

Forgiveness is the great need of this world because it is a world of illusions. Those who forgive are thus releasing themselves from illusions, whilst those who withhold forgiveness, are binding themselves to them.

So we may be able to reach a point in life when we experience ourselves as happy human beings without our addictive hits. In order to maintain this feeling, we need to maintain alert, mindful awareness, totally present from moment to moment. Contented feelings need to be cultivated in order to maintain a connection with our true being regardless of what is taking place in one's life. A day-to-day serenity and simplicity of life develops, detached from worldly and materialistic concerns. We need to just 'be' as each situation occurs and accept the routine of our lives without trying to enhance every moment with addictive thinking, addictive emotions and addictive behaviour. Only then are we able to feel and live the eternal moment of now; that is, reality as it occurs. We need to become a vigilant observer of negative feelings as they arise, as they are the signal that we have slipped into our conditioned past and deluded perception of self.

Master Hua-Ching Ni's statement 'One's life depends on oneself not on heaven' means spiritually responsible individuals allow God to work through them or surrender to a Higher Power; they experience a spiritual independence in touch with themselves and everyone else. A spiritual person is open to constant self-adjustment and vigilantly cultivates self-awareness based on feedback from others. The points of the triangle of how I see me, how others see me and who I really am begin to converge to a point focus, and the more in touch I am with my true or reality being. I know that I know that I know that I know, a knowingness or perceptive knowing, that I am at one with what is and at one with others. With this essence of inner knowing comes intuitiveness, followed by creativity and eventually inspiration. We finally come to realise our real truth and that our view of external reality is only a reflection of our internal reality. It is energy projected by our mind which creates the experience. The more stable and quiet the mind and body, the more comfortable the experience; the perception of the experience and the experience become one.

Allowing strong emotions of extreme happiness or extreme sadness to overwhelm us will create physical imbalances; emotional excess leads to addictive behaviours that damage our nervous system and metabolism. This can be temporary initially, but eventually can become pathological resulting in chronic addictions. Bad feelings, excessive emotion and impulsive behaviour are good indications that we are out of sync with reality and not in touch with the spiritual essence of our being. People often think that the mind is a place where they can enjoy freedom, even in difficult situations; this is a deluded escape. We can only attain freedom through liberation from our destructive emotions attached to our mythical self. The goal of self-cultivation is to experience stability, simplicity and true emotional freedom. We reach a stage when we no longer allow outside pressures to influence who we feel we are or intrude on our good feeling of just being. We become more balanced, lessening our desire for addictive behaviour.

So, how do we as addicts deal with normal daily pressures or pleasures without becoming overly emotional and returning to our addictive behaviour? The only way to prevent ourselves from sliding into ignorant thinking and a deluded sense of self is to remain acutely aware of our feelings and emotions. We need to surrender to the moment of 'what is' and let go of our self-importance. We no longer need to be trapped in a bubble of unreal concepts, beliefs and feelings, and a false identity out of sync with reality. In reality, there is only present moment conscious awareness. It is only then that we truly are because there is nothing else.

We can still experience loving relationships, job satisfaction, possessions and feelings but they must not be addictive; that is, possessive physical and/or emotional attachments to situations and things due to a misconception of who we think we are. Instead of strong, needy, greedy feelings of desire or aversion, we can experience a more blissful awareness that can be cultivated moment-to-moment until it becomes our being, who we truly are. We then find that only those of similar being, vibrating with the same true energy as us, will appear in our life. As stated by the Master Hua-Ching Ni:

> *There will always be cycles in life, ones you enjoy and ones you do not, but remember that the highs are built by the lows and vice versa.*

Life is built by each interesting moment, not by excitement stemming from our mythical self. We need not be so obsessed with making a living and judging others that we forget to live. From an unknown author:

> *Nothing can substitute for good relationships. Relationships are the final determinant of life's worth.... Don't get so involved with making a living that you don't make a life.... After death there's no second chance. You've got to get it right the first time. It is a foregone conclusion that you'll be blown off course. It's not fatal; it's just the way everything works.*

The moment I feel excitement or anxiety or both, I know I have moved out of my present moment into my mind, with its memory of past anxieties or excitements, and will project these same feelings into the future. This is not the way to live because I will slip rapidly into addictive thinking and return to my addiction. Spiritual enjoyment is never exhausted, whereas mental excitement exhausts real feelings of enjoyment and only leads to addictive behaviour.

If we allow our egos to control us, we exist on habit and our past. We need to be an observer of life and not become an emotional participant, attaching to every situation and thought. So do not resist the moment. Do not resist what is happening in the moment with judgemental thoughts and reactionary emotions. When an emotion arises within, know that it is resistance to the moment. Allow the gap of further thought and compounded emotion. Remain with and feel the current emotion, focus on the breath and bring awareness to the emotion and it will quickly dissipate. Try thinking of your emotions as clouds: they look solid but they're not; they change shape and disperse, move on and reform. Become aware of an inner calm; become aware when there is chaos around you; become aware when you feel stressed; become aware of how people's suffering affects you; become aware that your past conditioning is contaminating your present moment; become aware when your energy and body sensations are not in sync; and become aware when you feel any emotional discomfort.

A quote of the *A Course in Miracles* sums it up:

What if you recognised this world as an hallucination? What if you really understood you made it up? What if you realise that those who seem to walk about in it, to sin, die, attack and murder and destroy themselves are wholly unreal?

It is this active letting go of perceptions, judgements and emotions that allows the false view of self to dissolve and pure awareness of just being to manifest. This is true life, when we begin to realise how our habitual addictive living was only a compensation for our unreal and addictive feelings. Only we are responsible to work miracles so we can reach a stage of enlightenment or contentment in life, not based on any external condition, with the happy realisation of not needing to do anything to enhance the sense of me. Once the myth of past and future are gone, only the truth of past and future exist, not the myth of who we think we are in relation to our conditioned past and future.

We finally reach a feeling of knowing, an inner feeling of contented energy, regardless of what is going on around us. We are then living as a knowing being, knowing who we are. This calm inner energy of true being infiltrates our lives more and more, and we deal with outside impingements as 'a passing parade' without any emotional attachment. Thus we are more in touch with reality.

As quoted by Lama Yeshe in *Introduction to Tantra*:

It is the limited conceptualisation that prevents us from experiencing the explosion of blissful energy latent within our nervous system and therefore realising our potential for full enlightenment.

Two quotes from *A Course in Miracles*:

The 'I am' is the only truth and cannot be threatened. Everything else is unreal (my nightmare of illusion) and doesn't exist. 'Herein lies the peace of God' and only this is my reality.

Fantasies change realities. That is their purpose. They cannot do so in reality but they can do so in the mind that would have reality be different.

Personally, I think the above summarises it all. The only way to dissolve our mythical false self is to live in the present. Attachment to material possessions, analysing the past, reliving past emotional experiences, wishful day-dreaming and searching for security and continuity keeps us imprisoned in our false self, which is non-reality that supports our addictions and causes suffering. Trying to 'fix it' with various habitual medications from psychological to physiological causes us to experience even more unreal feelings, which are permanently in conflict with reality and cause even more suffering, hence the saying 'The truth shall set you free'. It is the knowing and living our true being that grants us freedom from suffering. If we observe the rising and dispersing of our emotions, we come to realise that each perception, thought and feeling is only temporary and merely passes through our true being without attachment and the need for a compensatory addictive behaviour.

I will finish with a quote from *A Course in Miracles*:

The quiet centre in which you do nothing will remain with you, giving you rest in the midst of every busy doing on which you are sent. Far from the centre you will be directed how to use the body sinlessly. And to have faith in this is to heal. It is a sign that you've accepted the atonement for yourself. You have given yourself the gift of freedom from the past, condemning no-one, neither yourself and just be in 'loving kindness'.

In summary…

- Freedom from our deluded self and accompanying destructive emotions and addictive behaviour only can be obtained by continuous mindful awareness, a vigilant awareness of any emotions as they arise.

- We practise staying with the emotion; we take responsibility for any potentially destructive emotion by delaying the emotion that could lead to a reactive and/or addictive behaviour. It is a mind-body intervention.

- We need to just 'be' as each situation occurs and accept the routine of our lives without trying to enhance every moment with addictive thinking, addictive emotions and addictive behaviour. Only then are we able to feel and live the eternal moment of now; that is, reality as it occurs.

Bibliography

Alcoholics Anonymous (1976). *Alcoholics Anonymous Big Book* (3rd edn). Alcoholics Anonymous World Services Inc.: New York City, pp. 58, 550.

American Psychiatric Association (1994). DSM IV Criteria for Addiction. *Diagnostic and Statistical Manual of Mental Health Disorders* (4th edn). American Psychiatric Association: Arlington, VA.

Bateson, Gregory (1971). The cybernetics of self: A theory of alcoholism. *Psychiatry*, vol. 34(1), pp. 1–18.

Benoit, Hubert (1998). *The Supreme Doctrine: Psychological Studies in Zen Thought*. Sussex Academic Press: East Sussex, UK.

Braden, Gregg (2000). *The Isaiah Effect: Decoding the Lost Science of Prayer and Prophecy*. Three Rivers Press: New York, p. 149.

Chopra, Deepak (2000). *How to Know God: The Soul's Journey into the Mystery of Mysteries*. Harmony Books, Crowe Publications: New York.

Chopra, Deepak (2004). *The Book of Secrets: Unlocking the Hidden Dimensions of Your Life*. Harmony Books, Random House: New York.

Chopra, Deepak (2006). *Power, Freedom and Grace: Living from the Source of Lasting Happiness*. Amber-Allen Publishing: San Rafael, CA.

Deepak, Chopra, Hay, Louise L., Dwyer, Wayne W., Collins, Terah K., Virtue, Doreen & Macson, Leon (2001). *Today's Wisdom*. Macson & Sons: Brighton Le Sands, Sydney, pp. 14-15.

Cleary, Thomas (2000). *Taoist Meditation: Methods for Cultivating a Healthy Mind and Body*. Shambhala: Boston/London, p. 27.

Coelho, Paulo (1999). *Veronika Decides to Die*. HarperCollins Publishers: London.

Dalai Lama, His Holiness the (1995). *Awakening the Mind: Lightening the Heart*. HarperCollins Publishers: New York.

Dalai Lama, His Holiness the (2002). *The Dalai Lama's Little Book of Wisdom*. HarperCollins Publishers: London.

Dalai Lama, His Holiness the & Cutler, Howard C. (1998). *The Art of Happiness: A Handbook for Living*. Riverhead Books, Penguin Group: New York.

Dawkins, Richard (1976). *The Selfish Gene*. Oxford University Press: London.

Foundation for Inner Peace (1996). *A Course in Miracles* (2nd edn). Viking, Penguin Books: New York, pp. x, xi.

Goleman, Daniel (2003). *Destructive Emotions: How Can We Overcome Them? A Scientific Dialogue with the Dalai Lama*. Bantam Books, Random House: London, pp. 75, 288.

Goleman, Daniel (2003). *Healing Emotions: Conversations with the Dalai Lama on Mindfulness, Emotions and Health*. Shambhala Books: Boston/London.

Hall, Calvin S. & Nordby, Vernon J. (1973). *A Primer of Jungian Psychology*. New American Library: New York, p. 54.

Jung, Carl G. (1970). *Flying Saucers: A Modern Myth of Things Seen in the Skies*. Princeton University Press: New York, p. 23.

Kabat-Zinn, Jon (1994). *Wherever You Go, There You Are*. Piatkus: London, p. 236.

Klein, Jean (1989). *I Am*. Third Millennium Publications: Guernsey, CI.

Lesser, Elizabeth (2004). *Broken Open: How Difficult Times Can Help Us Grow.* Rider, Random House: London, pp. 7, 117.

Lilienfield, Scott, Lynn, Steven, Ruscio, John & Bernstein, Barry (2010). Big myths in popular psychology. *Scientific American Mind*, March/April, p. 47.

McGraw, Phillip C. (2001). *Self Matters: Creating Your Life from the Inside Out.* Simon & Schuster Source: London.

Mason, Michael (1994). *William Blake Selected Poetry.* Oxford University Press: Oxford, p. 74.

Ni, Hua-Ching (1997). *Entering the Tao.* Shambhala Publications: Boston/London, pp. 20, 33, 45.

Peck, M. Scott (1983). *People of the Lie: The Hope for Healing Human Evil.* Cox & Wyman: Berkshire, UK.

Peck, M. Scott (1983). *The Road Less Traveled.* Hutchinson, Random House: London, p. 3.

Peck, M. Scott (1990). *The Different Drum: Community Making and Peace.* Random House: London.

Peck, M. Scott (1993). *Further Along the Road Less Traveled: The Unending Journey Toward Spiritual Growth.* Touchstone: New York, p. 63.

Powell, Robert (1983). *The Great Awakening: Reflections on Zen and Reality.* Theosophical Publishing House: Wheaton, IL, pp. 4, 5, 23, 30, 40, 50, 59, 122.

Suzuki, David, McConnell, Amanda & Mason, Adrienne (2008). *The Sacred Balance: Rediscovering Our Place in Nature* (revised edn). Allen & Unwin: Sydney.

Tolle, Eckhart (1999). *The Power of Now: A Guide to Spiritual Enlightenment.* Griffin Press: Adelaide, pp. 23, 49, 191.

Tolle, Eckhart (2003). *Stillness Speaks.* Hodder Stoughton: London, pp. 52–53.

Tolle, Eckhart (2005). *A New Earth: Awakening to Your Life's Purpose.* Penguin Group: Melbourne.

Urschel, Harold C. (2009). *Healing the Addicted Brain: The Revolutionary Science-Based Alcoholism and Addiction Recovery Program.* Sourcebooks Inc.: Naperville, IL, p. 26.

Watts, Alan (1966). *The Tao of Philosophy.* Tuttle Publishing: Boston, MA.

Witteveen, Hendrikus J. (2005). *Sufism In Action.* Vega: London.

Yeshe, Thubten & Landaw, Jonathan (1987). *Introduction to Tantra: A Vision of Totality.* Wisdom Publications: Boston, MA, pp. 54, 55, 75, 77.